The Third Reich
Demise of the Nazi Dream

Titles in the History's Great Defeats series include:

The Third Reich
Demise of the Nazi Dream

by Earle Rice Jr.

Lucent Books, San Diego, CA

Library of Congress Cataloging-in-Publication Data

Rice, Earle.
    The fall of the Third Reich : demise of the Nazi dream / by Earle Rice Jr.
      p. cm. — (History's great defeats)
    Includes bibliographical references and index.
    Summary: Describes the rise and fall of Nazi Germany and explores
the philosophical, economic, and military principles on which it was based.
    ISBN 1-56006-630-X (alk. paper)
    1. Germany—History—1933–1945—Juvenile literature. 2. National
socialism—Juvenile literature. 3. Hitler, Adolf, 1889–1945—Biography
—Juvenile literature. 4. World War, 1939–1945—Germany—Juvenile
literature. 5. Jews—Persecutions—Germany—History—20th Century
—Juvenile literature. [1. Germany—History—1933–1945. 2. National
—socialism.] I. Title. II. Series.

DD256.5 .R472   2000
943.086—dc21
                                    99-046869

Cover: A Russian soldier raises a flag over the Reichstag in 1945.

Table of Contents

Foreword

Ⲓ N 334 B.C., ALEXANDER, king of Macedonia, led his small but formidable Greek army into Asia. In the short span of only ten years, he brought Persia, the largest empire the world had yet seen, to its knees, earning him the nickname forever after associated with his name—"the Great." The demise of Persia, which at its height stretched from the shores of the Mediterranean Sea in the west to the borders of India in the east, was one of history's most stunning defeats. It occurred primarily because of some fatal flaws in the Persian military system, disadvantages the Greeks had exploited before, though never as spectacularly as they did under Alexander.

First, though the Persians had managed to conquer many peoples and bring huge territories under their control, they had failed to create an individual fighting man who could compare with the Greek hoplite. A heavily armored infantry soldier, the hoplite carried a thrusting spear and short sword and fought in a highly effective and lethal battlefield formation—the phalanx. Possessed of better armor, weapons, and training than the Persians, Alexander's soldiers repeatedly crushed their Persian opponents. Second, the Persians for the most part lacked generals of the caliber of their Greek counterparts. And when Alexander invaded, Persia had the added and decisive disadvantage of facing one of the greatest generals of all time. For these reasons, the fate of a great empire was sealed and it disappeared forever.

Other world powers and civilizations have fallen in a like manner. They have succumbed to some combination of inherent fatal flaws or disadvantages, to political and/or military mistakes, and even to the personal failings of their leaders.

Another of history's great defeats was the sad demise of the North American Indian tribes at the hands of encroaching white civilization from the sixteenth to nineteenth centuries. In this case, all of the tribes suffered from the same crippling disadvantages. Among the worst, they lacked the great numbers, the unity, and the advanced industrial and military hardware possessed by the whites. Still another example, one closer to our own time, was the resounding defeat of Nazi Germany by the Allies in 1945, which brought World War II, the most disastrous conflict in history, to a close. Nazi Germany collapsed for many reasons. But one of the most telling was that its leader, Adolf Hitler, sorely underestimated the material resources and human resolve of the Allies, especially the United States. In the end, Germany was in a very real sense submerged by a massive and seemingly relentless tidal wave of Allied bombs, tanks, ships, and soldiers.

Seen in retrospect, a good many of the fatal flaws, drawbacks, and mistakes that caused these and other great defeats from the pages of history seem to stand out as glaring and obvious. It is only natural to wonder why, in each case, the loser did not realize its limitations and/or errors sooner and attempt to avert disaster. But closer examination of the events, social and political trends, and leading personalities involved usually reveals that complex factors were at play. Overconfidence, arrogance, fear, ignorance, stubbornness, innocence, and other all too human attitudes held by nations, peoples, and individuals often colored and shaped their reactions, goals, and strategies. And it is both fascinating and instructive to reconstruct how such attitudes, as well as the fatal flaws and mistakes themselves, contributed to the loser's ultimate demise.

Each volume in Lucent Books' *History's Great Defeats* series is designed to provide the reader with diverse learning tools for exploring the topic at hand. Each well-informed, clearly written text is supported and enlivened by substantial quotes by the actual people involved, as well as by later historians and other experts; and these primary and secondary sources are carefully documented. Each volume also supplies the reader with an extensive Works Consulted list, guiding him or her to further research on the topic. These and other research tools, including glossaries and time lines, afford the reader a thorough understanding of how and why one of history's most decisive defeats occurred and how these events shaped our world.

The Nazis and
Introduction # Their Dream

A state which in this day of racial poisoning dedicates itself to the care of its best racial elements must some day become lord of the earth.

—Adolf Hitler, *Mein Kampf*

A T NOON ON JANUARY 30, 1933, Paul von Hindenburg, the aging second president of the Weimar Republic, appointed Adolf Hitler chancellor of Germany and the Third Reich was born. Six hours later, commencing at about dusk, thousands of storm troopers carrying torches and singing the "Horst Wessel Lied" ("Horst Wessel Song," official marching song of the Nazi Party) and other martial songs paraded through the streets of Berlin in celebration of the new chancellor (chief minister of state) and the prospect of a German-ruled "New Order" in Europe.

The procession continued well past midnight. Tens of thousands of disciplined troops poured from the depths of the Tiergarten (park) and passed under the triumphal arch of the Brandenburg Gate. Their raised torches formed a moving canopy of flame that brightened the night and kindled the spirits of the masses lining the sidewalks along the parade route. "Hurrahs!" and shouts of "Heil, Heil, Sieg Heil!" ("Sieg Heil!" means "Hail to Victory!") resonated again and again in the chill night air. Trumpets blared, cymbals clashed, and drums boomed. Column after column of brown-shirted, jackbooted troops tramped in thundering unison down the Wilhelmstrasse, past the presidential palace, and on past the chancellery.

Above the thoroughfare Adolf Hitler, joyful and wildly excited, stood at an open window in the chancellery, smiling and laughing and jabbing his arm perpetually skyward in the stiff Nazi salute. Tears of elation streamed freely from his eyes. Franz von Papen, his vice chancellor, viewed the marchers over Hitler's shoulder. Hitler turned to him and spoke with a voice choked with emotion. "What an immense task we have set ourselves, Herr von Papen—we must never part until our work is accomplished."[1]

On the boulevard below, somewhere among the teeming masses, young Melita Maschmann witnessed the martial spectacular with her parents. Years later, she wrote:

> Some of the uncanny feeling of that night remains with me even today. The crashing tread of the feet, the somber pomp of the red and black [swastika] flags, the flickering light from the torches on the faces and the songs with melodies that were at once aggressive and sentimental.[2]

Perhaps the seeming contradictions in the martial music some-how reflected a feeling shared by many Germans at that time: hope that under Hitler's guidance Germany would soon regain its pre–World War I prominence and respect in the world community, and a

Newly appointed German chancellor Adolf Hitler (center) stands with senior members of the Nazi Party in 1933.

fear that his leadership might instead plunge Germany into the abyss of another destructive world conflict.

In the eyes of most foreign observers, a renewal of German militarism signaled only trouble in the days ahead. French ambassador André François-Poncet, who witnessed the Nazi extravaganza in Berlin, wrote, "The river of fire flowed past the French Embassy, whence, with heavy heart and filled with foreboding, I watched its luminous wake."[3]

Joseph Goebbels, who had personally arranged the Nazi victory parade and was soon to become the Third Reich's Minister for Public Enlightenment and Propaganda, ended the eventful evening in a happier—even giddy—frame of mind. In an early morning entry in his diary, he scribbled: "It is almost like a dream . . . a fairy tale. . . . The new Reich has been born. Fourteen years of work have been crowned with victory. The German revolution has begun."[4]

Dreams sometimes do come true. In March 1933 the Nazi Party gained a majority in the Reichstag (German parliament) and a new breed of Germans seized control of the nation. Under the singular,

---

 ## Missed Opportunities

In 1932 Heinrich Brüning, chancellor of the German Weimar Republic, failed to act on two opportunities to smash the rival Nazis. André François-Poncet, then French ambassador in Berlin, later wrote of these lost opportunities. Here, he is quoted in *Hitler's Diplomat* by John Weitz:

> Brüning's errors were typically German. He did not realize that the praise he got abroad rendered him suspect at home. He never realized to what pitch of blind fanaticism nationalist passion might rise, a frenzy too fierce to be assuaged by any victories he might have won. He tried the velvet glove. The Germans preferred the mailed fist. He was repelled by the drastic and brutal methods which would have saved him. He had two excellent opportunities to smash the Nazis: they were twice discovered planning treason and insurrection. Arms were found and plans for a coup d'état. Everything could be proved. But Brüning would not smash his opponents.

After the Nazi Party won majorities in the next regional elections, President Paul von Hindenburg withdrew his support for Brüning. Brüning resigned on May 30, 1932.

Joseph Goebbels called the rise of the Third Reich the start of a "German revolution."

all-powerful rule of Adolf Hitler, they set about at once to make the Nazi dream—the *fairy tale*—come true. And the world watched in silence as the dream became a dreadful reality.

The Nazi Dream

The Nazis saw themselves as members of a racially pure master race and dreamed of dominating the world. Their dream—some might say delusion—grew out of Adolf Hitler's conception of the world and philosophy of life, often expressed in the lexicon of the Third Reich as *Weltanschauung*, or worldview.

Hitler, the principal founder of National Socialism, or Nazism, was born in Austria in 1889, the son of a minor customs official. In World War I, serving as a corporal in the Bavarian army, he was gassed, wounded, and twice decorated for bravery. The outcome of the war embittered Hitler, and much of his worldview was shaped by his abiding hatred for Jews and Marxists, both of whom he blamed for Germany's humiliating defeat and subsequent economic collapse.

Hitler (front row, far left) was twice honored for his bravery as a World War I corporal.

He later wrote, "If we pass all the causes of the German collapse in review, the ultimate and most decisive [cause] remains the failure to recognize the racial problem and especially the Jewish menace."[5]

In 1920, at the age of thirty, Hitler settled in Munich and soon joined with fellow nationalists to form the Nazi Party. He quickly advanced to party leadership, all the while advocating policies of racial hatred and extreme nationalism. (Nazi is an acronym from *NAtional-soZIalist;* the party name was meant to imply a blend of nationalism and socialism for broad appeal, while masking the party's purely fascist ideology.) Hitler and his Nazi disciples dedicated themselves to restoring German pride in self and country, no small task in a nation humbled by the harsh limits and reparations imposed on Germany under the terms of the Treaty of Versailles that ended World War I.

Three years later, after a failed attempt to overthrow the Bavarian government (the famous Beer Hall Putsch), Hitler was arrested and incarcerated in Landsberg am Lech, a fortress prison in Bavaria. While serving nine months of a five-year sentence, he wrote *Mein Kampf* (My Struggle), dictating much of it to fellow inmate Rudolf Hess, who would one day serve as his chief deputy. The autobiographical work is a rambling, semiliterate diatribe filled with anti-Semitism, power worship, gross immoralities, and a detailed plan for world domination. This handbook of evil became the bible of the Nazi Party.

Upon his release from prison under an amnesty in 1924, Hitler set right to work rebuilding the Nazi Party, which had temporarily disbanded after the Munich putsch. Aided by two close followers, Dr. Paul Joseph Goebbels, a lame, slightly built propaganda specialist, and Hermann Göring, a hulking World War I flying ace, Hitler undertook the tough task of winning mass support for his National Socialist policies. By then Hitler's doctrines of race and living space (*Lebensraum*)—the two basic canons of Nazism—were solidly rooted in the party's *Weltanschauung*. To these twin doctrines Hitler added a third tenet: the *Führerprinzip*, the leadership principle.

The *Führerprinzip*, outlined by Hitler in *Mein Kampf*, mandated an authoritarian government for the new Germany, with power emanating from the supreme leader. He disdained democracy as nonsense and clearly advocated a dictatorship. "Every man will have

Hitler's failed attempt to overthrow the Bavarian government earned him nine months in prison.

helpers to advise him, but the decision will be made by one man [*Der Führer*, or the leader]," [6] Hitler declared. There would be no parliamentarian rule in the Third Reich—only a leader with absolute power and an elite of assistant leaders. This principle was applied in descending order to all organizations within the Nazi hierachy.

Entwined, the loathsome doctrines of race and space became the essence of Hitler's worldview. The leadership principle provided a means to his nefarious aims. Together they became the stuff the Nazi dream was made of.

The "Thousand-Year Reich"

In 1929, aided by an economic depression and their mastery of deceitful strategy (which they called the "big lie"), the Nazi dream merchants sold these three concepts to enough Germans to win the support of the workers and the bankers and industrialists. Hitler, calling on his frenzied but charismatic oratorial skills and his astute knowledge of mass psychology, preached his hateful doctrines of race and space over and again, always emphasizing Germany's need for a solitary leader.

His doctrines of race and space derived from his belief in a perverted form of social Darwinism, under which individuals and nations are thought to be engaged in an ongoing struggle for life. Thus Hitler warned that the supposedly racially superior Germans—ostensibly purebreds of Nordic or Aryan stock—were threatened from within by Jews and others of what he considered impure blood.

"Human culture and civilization on this continent are inseparably bound up with the presence of the Aryan," Hitler declared in *Mein Kampf* (which by 1939 had sold more than 5.2 million copies, making its author a rich man).

> If he [the supposedly culturally superior Aryan] dies out or declines [presumedly through interracial unions and crossbreeding with Jews and others of impure bloodlines], the dark veils of an age without culture will again descend on this globe. [7]

Hitler saw Jews and their influence at the core of all of Germany's (and indeed the world's) problems. Karl Marx, founder of modern socialism and communism, was a Jew. Jews controlled trade unions, international banking, the press, the arts, social morals, and

Hitler used his anti-Semitic autobiography, Mein Kampf *(pictured), to espouse his plans for world domination.*

virtually every other aspect of German life. "Was there any form of filth or profligacy, particularly in cultural life, without at least one Jew involved in it?"[8] Hitler asked. Germany, he railed, could regain its past greatness only by waging unrelenting warfare against these internal enemies.

Addressing external issues, Hitler pledged that a new, powerful Germany under a National Socialist government would extend Germany's borders to fit its population by the conquest of additional *Lebensraum*, or living space. Native populations of conquered lands, he said, would be expelled or exterminated but in no case assimilated. Lands acquired in this fashion would be made available to fine, virile Nordic couples to settle on and perpetuate their race. The resultant population gain would not only replace casualties incurred in the conquest of these lands; it would also make available additional military manpower for future German expansion. Today Europe, Hitler conjectured, tomorrow the world.

Renewed Hope

On the night of January 30, 1933, many Germans greeted Hitler's appointment as Germany's chancellor with hope for a better future. In *Adolf Hitler*, biographer and historian John Toland records one storm trooper's remembrance of that eventful night:

> Everyone felt the same—that things will get better. Although realistically there was no reason for them to believe things would improve, they believed it. They had hope again. It was remarkable. I don't think that Germany will ever again find another man who could inspire as much hope, trust and love as Hitler did at that moment.

Hitler's appointment as chancellor filled many Germans with optimism for the future.

Once in power, Hitler worked rapidly to consolidate his dictatorial powers, combining legislation with a reign of brutality and terror to achieve his ends. On August 12, 1934, upon the death of the aging and failing President von Hindenburg, Hitler took the last step in his march to absolute power. Refusing to wear the mantle of *Reichspresident* (Reich president), he declared himself both *Kanzler* (chancellor) and *Der Führer* of the Third Reich, which he boasted would last for a thousand years. Hitler vastly overestimated the Third Reich's staying power: it lasted slightly longer than twelve years.

Factors in the Fall

Many factors contributed to the fall of Hitler's Reich and the demise of the Nazi dream. Singling out one circumstance or event as the chief factor in Germany's defeat would be at best to invite contradiction and at worst to misrepresent history. As the truth usually lies somewhere between two extremes, a careful examination of several key factors is necessary to understand why the Third Reich failed.

These factors include Hitler's personal failings, flawed alliances, war on two fronts, despicable diversions, misuse of technology, economic warfare, and the lack of moral authority among the Third Reich's leaders. Taken together, these factors leave little doubt as to why the Third Reich crumbled and Germany lost the war.

Ten years before Hitler seized power in Germany, he wrote, *"Germany will either be a world power or there will be no Germany."* [9] In the latter sense, he was almost right.

Hitler's Leadership: Mistakes on a Grand Scale

Chapter 1

No one doubts that the war was ultimately Hitler's responsibility, or that Hitler made mistakes on a grand scale. In most postwar explanations of the outcome Hitler's failings stand at the head of the list.

—Richard Overy, *Why the Allies Won*

ADOLF HITLER WAS ONE of the most extraordinary individuals of the twentieth century. As the absolute ruler of Nazi Germany, he lifted his nation from the depths of national humiliation and economic depression and launched Germany on the path to world domination, ethnic and racial genocide, and ultimate self-destruction. Almost single-handedly, he started World War II—the widest-ranging, most destructive war in human history: a war that in the end claimed the lives of more than 50 million people. Possibly, Adolf Hitler was also the most evil individual of the twentieth century.

Some novelists have written books depicting what life might have been like had Germany won the war. The unsettling truth is that Germany came close to winning World War II. Some students of history conclude that a strong case can be made that the Allies did not *win* the war, but rather that the Germans *lost* it. Ironically, nothing contributed more to Germany's downfall than Hitler's own failings.

"ALL POWERS IN THE FÜHRER'S HANDS"

In the last analysis, Hitler was a colossal failure but an incredibly clever and devious one. No other world leader so completely dominated his nation's war effort as did Adolf Hitler. His ideas and policies on domestic, foreign, and military affairs infused every facet of German life in the late 1930s and throughout the war years.

His role as unrestrained war leader stemmed from a series of shrewdly crafted political manipulations following his appointment as chancellor. In 1934, acting now as *Der Führer* of the Third Reich, he prohibited all other political parties and began ruling with emergency dictatorial powers. Over the next three years, he positioned loyal Nazis in prominent state positions and eliminated by dismissal or assassination those whom he felt a threat to his leadership. He repudiated the Treaty of Versailles in March 1935 and began an accelerated rearmament program in Germany.

In 1936 Hitler sent troops into the Rhineland—a demilitarized zone established by the Versailles treaty along the Rhine River—and reclaimed it for Germany in his first expansionist move. Hitler had so far repeatedly expressed his desire for peace, while privately he spoke of the "duty to war"[10] to those closest to him.

As early as February 1933, he had told his generals that Germany's new arms would be used "for the conquest and ruthless Germanization of new living space [*Lebensraum*] in the East."[11] But it was not until November 5, 1937, at a secret meeting held at the Reich Chancellery, that Hitler outlined his step-by-step plans for achieving living space by force and his blueprint for Germanizing conquered

In defiance of the Treaty of Versailles, rows of German tanks occupy the demilitarized zone in the Rhineland.

territories, beginning with Austria and Czechoslovakia. (The meeting became known as the Hossbach Conference. It was named for Hitler's military adjutant Friedrich Hossbach, who recorded what Hitler said and issued the highly secret Hossbach Memorandum five days later.) Hitler's plans stunned the military leaders, who feared that such actions would provoke a war at a time when Germany was still unprepared for a major conflict.

Hitler headed off any potential army resistance to his plans by firing two of his top generals and generally shaking up the Wehrmacht (German army) officer corps. Then, on February 4, 1938, he decreed: "From now on I take over personally the command of the whole armed forces." [12] As head of state, he already held the rank of supreme commander of the armed forces. But in this move he also assumed the post of army commander in chief (having fired the previous commander in chief) and abolished the War Ministry.

At the same time, Hitler created the *Oberkommando der Wehrmacht,* or OKW—the high command of the armed forces—and appointed himself as its supreme commander and Field Marshal Wilhelm Keitel as its chief. This revamped command structure subordinated the army, the navy, and the air force to the OKW and thus to Hitler. He now stood alone at the top of both the military and government hierarchies of Germany. From this time on, no major affairs of state could be carried out without Hitler's knowledge and approval.

The next day, February 5, headlines emblazoned in the *Völkischer Beobachter* (Racial Observer), the leading Nazi newspaper, heralded: "STRONGEST CONCENTRATION OF ALL POWERS IN THE FÜHRER'S HANDS!" [13]

At last, as the unassailable supreme dictator of the Third Reich, Adolf Hitler now stood poised to turn his dream of expanding Germany's living space into reality.

Hitler's Greatest Mistake

In a series of brazen moves against neighboring European states, Hitler annexed Austria in March 1938 and at the Munich Conference in September 1938 bluffed Great Britain and France into ceding him the Sudetenland (the German-speaking frontier areas of Czechoslovakia). In March 1939 he occupied the Czech provinces of Bohemia and Moravia, declared Slovakia a protectorate, handed over Ruthenia (a

German police march past supporters of the Third Reich as Austria is annexed in 1938.

former autonomous region and later province of Czechoslovakia but now the Zakarpats'ka subdivision in the Ukraine) to Hungary, and reclaimed the previously German-owned Baltic region of Memelland from Lithuania.

This string of bloodless triumphs won Hitler widespread popular support at home and stoked the fires of his growing sense of invincibility. The newly acquired lands also fed vital material resources into Hitler's rearmament program, which he hoped would make Germany the major military power in Europe by the early or mid-1940s. Moreover, the lack of opposition to his land-grabbing moves convinced Hitler that the Versailles signatory nations would not oppose further German expansions to the east. He now cast a covetous eye toward Poland and the port city of Danzig (Gdansk), which had been stripped from Germany following World War I, along with a narrow strip of land called the Polish Corridor, to provide Poland with an outlet to the Baltic Sea.

Hitler, it turned out, had miscalculated. On March 31, contrary to Hitler's convictions, British prime minister Neville Chamberlain announced in the House of Commons that Britain would guarantee Poland's security and territorial integrity. France soon echoed

British prime minister Neville Chamberlain enraged Hitler by vowing to protect Poland from Nazi advances.

Britain's pledge, even though neither nation was militarily prepared to go to war. When the news reached Hitler, he flew into a rage and vowed, "I'll cook them a stew they'll choke on!"[14]

On April 3 Hitler issued a new directive to his military chiefs, broadening his earlier plans for seizing Danzig. The new plan—*Fall Weiss* (Case White)—called for the invasion of Poland and the destruction of the Polish armed forces. The date for the invasion was set for September 1, 1939.

The following month, Hitler hedged his bets by entering into a political alliance with Italy in Berlin on May 22. Italian dictator Benito Mussolini called the alliance the Pact of Steel. Its terms stipulated that Germany and Italy would "act side by side and with united forces to secure their living space," and that each nation would "immediately" aid the other militarily should either country become "involved in warlike complications."[15]

Hitler's generals frowned on the alliance, but Hitler and Mussolini both wanted it—each for different reasons: Mussolini, his nation militarily ill-prepared, wanted to stave off a major European war, so he signed the agreement with the verbal understanding that neither nation would provoke a war before 1943. Hitler, about to invade Poland, sought to ensure a successful outcome to his venture by tying Germany's fortunes to those of a nation that he mistakenly believed to be a formidable power.

On May 23 Hitler announced his future foreign plans to fourteen senior officers representing all three branches of the German military. He emphasized that war was unavoidable:

> Further successes cannot be gained without the shedding of blood. . . . It is a question of expanding our living space in the east. . . . There is no question of sparing Poland and we are left with the decision: to attack Poland at the first suitable opportunity. We cannot expect a repetition of the Czech affair [a bloodless takeover]. There will be war. Our task is to isolate Poland.

But Hitler left no doubt as to his willingness to take on Britain and France—or even the Soviet Union—should they interfere with his military operations:

> The aim must be to deal the enemy a smashing or a finally decisive blow right at the start. Considerations of right or wrong, or of treaties, do not enter into the matter. . . . Preparations must be made for a long war as well as for a surprise attack, and every possible intervention by England on the Continent must be smashed.[16]

Hitler and Italian dictator Benito Mussolini formed their Pact of Steel alliance just months before the start of World War II.

"A Man of Reason"

When Hitler announced plans for invading Poland to fourteen of his top generals on May 23, 1939, not a single general protested. Not one feared that further German aggression would foment a war in Europe. In the following excerpt from Matthew Cooper's *The German Army, 1933–1945*, Field Marshal Erich von Manstein explains why:

> We had watched Germany's precarious course along the razor's edge to date with close attention and were increasingly amazed at Hitler's incredible luck in attaining . . . all his overt and covert aims. The man seemed to have an almost infallible instinct. Success had followed success. . . . All those things had been achieved without war. Why, we asked ourselves, should it be different this time? Look at Czechoslovakia. . . . [W]e recalled Hitler's assertion that he would never be so rash as to unleash a war on two fronts. . . . That at least implied a man of reason. . . . [H]e had explicitly assured his military advisers that he was not idiot enough to bungle his way into a world war for the sake of Danzig [Gdansk] or the Polish Corridor.

Not one officer at the meeting raised a dissenting voice. Less than three weeks later, the *Oberkommando des Heeres*, or OKH—the high command of the army—handed plans for the army's operations against Poland to Hitler.

On August 23, little more than a week before the scheduled start of the invasion, Hitler stunned Europe and the rest of the Western world by signing a nonaggression pact with Germany's adversary, the Soviet Union. Popularly known as the Hitler-Stalin Pact, it contained secret clauses for partitioning Poland between the two nations. This alliance between two avowed enemies was a stunning coup for Hitler. "Now," he proclaimed, "I have the world in my pocket!"[17]

The pact provided *temporary* advantages to both parties: from Hitler's viewpoint, it negated the prospect of Soviet intervention and therefore the threat of a second front, if Britain and France should honor their pledge to aid Poland; from Stalin's perspective, it provided a huge zone of Soviet influence and a buffer against would-be Western aggressors. Understandably, the agreement alarmed Britain and France.

In London, British prime minister Neville Chamberlain reiterated his nation's commitment to Poland, declaring, "Whatever may prove to be the nature of the German-Soviet agreement, it cannot alter Great Britain's obligations."[18] Nonetheless, the pact doomed Poland.

If Hitler took Chamberlain seriously, the dictator's words betrayed little sign of it. He spoke disparagingly of the British and the French. "I have met the umbrella men [diplomats]," he said. "The coffee sippers in London and Paris will stay this time, too. A world war will never, never, never come out of Case White."[19] Hitler is known to have gravely underestimated his adversaries many times, but perhaps never more so than on this occasion.

On September 1, 1939, in the hours before dawn, German air, sea, and land forces launched a violent assault on Poland. Two days later, Britain and France declared war on Germany. Hitler had misread the courage of the Western powers and their resolve to honor their commitment to Poland. His error in judgment touched off World

A motorcade of German troops advances through Poland. Germany's September 1, 1939, assault on Poland ignited World War II.

War II. In the years to come, Hitler would make many more mistakes but none so great as this one.

Hitler Errs Again

Adolf Hitler saw himself as a military genius and exercised fully his absolute authority to make strategic decisions that often ended in disasters. He certainly enjoyed some successes, however, as the Nazi war machine introduced the concept of blitzkrieg, or lightning war, to the practice of modern warfare. In only ten months, his motorized infantry and panzer (tank) forces, supported by the Luftwaffe (German air force), smashed through Poland, Denmark, part of Norway, Belgium, Luxembourg, Holland, and France.

Hitler claimed total credit for the success of these early victories during 1939–40. "I have again and again read Colonel [Charles] de Gaulle's [military leader and future president of France] book on methods of modern warfare employing fully motorized units," he told Albert Speer and others, "and I have learned a great deal from it."[20] But after his conquest of France, the führer's decisions began to go awry. Once again, Hitler underestimated the British.

With the Wehrmacht and Luftwaffe poised on the coast of the English Channel, Hitler expected Britain to sue for peace. When Britain instead elected, in the words of new British prime minister Winston Churchill, to "fight on unconquerable until the curse of Hitler is lifted from the brows of mankind,"[21] Hitler reluctantly started preparations for Operation Sea Lion—the invasion of Britain. But the Luftwaffe, under Reich Marshal Hermann Göring, failed to win air superiority in the air battle over Britain, forcing Hitler to postpone his invasion plans in September 1940.

Germany's air campaign against Britain was not only unsuccessful but costly as well. German aircraft losses totaled 1,733 shot down compared to 915 British. Moreover, Hitler's spiteful decision to switch the weight of German bombing attacks from fighter airfields and aircraft production plants to London and other cities contributed greatly to the Luftwaffe's unsuccessful campaign against the Royal Air Force. By diverting his bombers from British airfields and aircraft factories to the cities, Hitler enabled Britain to keep enough fighter planes flying to turn back the Luftwaffe. Without control of the air, Hitler was forced to postpone his planned invasion of Britain. Hitler had erred again.

German aircraft maneuver over London during the Third Reich's unsuccessful air campaign.

Hitler Blunders in the East

Undeterred by his costly losses over Britain, Hitler turned eastward and fixed his attention on what he considered the last essential step to achieving his *Lebensraum* dream—the invasion and dismantling of the Soviet Union. At 7:00 A.M. on June 22, 1941, propaganda minister Joseph Goebbels read a proclamation by Hitler over the radio: "I have decided again today to place the fate and future of the Reich and our people in the hands of our soldiers."[22] And with that announcement, Hitler launched Operation Barbarossa—the invasion of the Soviet Union—with full blitzkrieg fury.

The Hitler-Stalin Pact went by the boards in a classic breach of trust. By December 2 Hitler's panzers had driven to within sight of the Kremlin in Moscow, only to become mired in their tracks by the earliest and coldest Russian winter in half a century. Four days later, Hitler conceded that further progress was impossible. He told Alfred Jodl, his chief of operations, that "victory could no longer be achieved"[23] and canceled further offensive operations until the following spring.

The battle for Moscow resulted in Germany's first major land defeat of the war and was the turning point along the entire central front. Germany was now committed to a prolonged war and forced to fight on at least two fronts. The war on the Eastern Front remained stalemated until the Soviets took the offensive in March 1943. Operation Barbarossa—conceived and directed by Hitler himself—ranks as the German leader's greatest strategic blunder.

Hitler Guarantees Germany's Defeat

On December 7, 1941, the day after Hitler conceded defeat in the battle for Moscow, he received startling news at his field headquarters in Rastenburg, East Prussia, known as the *Wolfsschanze,* or Wolf's Lair. Shortly before midnight, a press officer rushed into Hitler's bunker with word of Japan's attack on the American naval base at Pearl Harbor. Hitler slapped his thighs delightedly and said, "The turning point! Now it is impossible for us to lose the war; we now have an ally who has never been vanquished in three thousand years, and another ally [Italy] who has been constantly vanquished but always ended up on the right side." [24]

Within a few days of hearing of the attack on Pearl Harbor, Hitler made another mistake. In September 1940 Germany, Italy, and Japan had signed the Tripartite Pact, which promised mutual aid if any one of its signers was attacked by a nation not already involved in the European war or in the war that Japan was then waging in China. Since Japan had attacked the United States rather than the other way around, Hitler was not bound by the pact's terms to render aid to Japan. Nevertheless, Hitler declared war on the United States on December 11. At a time when his armies had been brought to a standstill in the east by the Russian winter and the world's second strongest military nation, Hitler now boldly challenged the world's most economically powerful country. To his foreign minister, Joachim von Ribbentrop, Hitler justified what most observers viewed as an act of sheer lunacy this way:

> If we don't stand on the side of Japan, the pact is politically dead. But that is not the main reason. The chief reason is that the United States already is shooting at our ships. They have been a forceful factor in this war and through their actions have already created a condition of war. [25]

But by taking on the United States as an adversary, Hitler added another blunder to his fast-growing list of monumental mistakes and thereby guaranteed Germany's ultimate defeat.

The Turning Point

Despite Hitler's aberrant leadership, the year 1942 appeared to favor his cause. In North Africa, Field Marshal Erwin Rommel's Afrika Korps, which the British Eighth Army had contained in December 1941, commenced a new spring offensive in Libya. The famed "Desert Fox" captured the city of Tobruk in May and crossed into Egypt in June. His panzers drove to within seventy miles of Cairo before the British regrouped under the new command of General Bernard Montgomery and halted the German advance at El Alamein.

Meanwhile, at sea, Britain's losses in North Africa paled in the light of the enormous losses being inflicted on its supply lines in the Atlantic by the unrelenting attacks of Hitler's submarine (*Untersee-boot*, or U-boat) fleet. In the first half of 1942 alone, U-boats sank more than 4.5 million tons of Allied (British-U.S.-Soviet) shipping.

At the same time, German military fortunes improved on the Eastern Front. An ill-conceived Soviet thrust toward Kharkov in April, led by Marshal Semyon Timoshenko, almost neutralized the Red Army's offensive capability. The Germans trapped the overextended Soviet forces between two German armies and wiped out almost a quarter of a million Soviets. Farther south, Lieutenant General Andrey Vlasov lost his entire Second Shock Army in an abortive attack on German positions in the Crimea. Hitler, elated by his armies' successes, moved his military headquarters from Rastenburg to Winniza, in the Ukraine, and took personal command of field operations from July 17 through October 31.

On July 21, in an upbeat directive to his commanders, Hitler wrote:

> The unexpectedly rapid and favorable development of the operations against the Timoshenko Army Group entitles us to assume that we may soon succeed in depriving Soviet Russia of the Caucasus, with her most important source of oil, and of a valuable line of communication for the delivery of English and American supplies.[26]

Two days later, the German Sixth Army Group seized Rostov-on-Don, and its panzers were cranking hard toward what would become the fateful attack on Stalingrad.

The German assault on Stalingrad commenced on August 19. But after two months of savage fighting, the Soviets mounted a strong counterattack, isolating and slowly obliterating most of General Friedrich von Paulus's German Sixth Army. The führer refused to admit that the siege of Stalingrad had failed, however. As late as January 25, 1943, a pitiless Hitler ordered:

> Surrender is forbidden. Sixth Army will hold their position to the last man and last round, and by their heroic endurance will make an unforgettable contribution toward the establishment of a defensive front and the salvation of the Western World.[27]

Despite his führer's orders, Paulus surrendered what remained of his Sixth Army on January 31, 1943, forcing Hitler to abandon the Caucasus. Hitler had once again underestimated the power and fortitude of his enemy. The Germans' devastating defeat at Stalingrad marked the turning point of the war on the Eastern Front.

Hitler in Defeat

Once the tide of war turned against Hitler and the Germans in 1943, it never receded. Anglo-American forces threw Rommel's Afrika Korps out of North Africa in June, conquered Sicily in August, and advanced halfway up the Italian peninsula by year's end. Meanwhile, in July the Italians had deposed Hitler's friend and fellow dictator Mussolini. Two months later, Italy made peace with the Allies, leaving the Germans to fight alone in Italy.

On June 6, 1944, the Allies launched their long-awaited invasion of western Europe at Normandy and advanced almost to the Rhine by December. Hitler mounted a last offensive in the Ardennes, which the Allies repulsed in the Battle of the Bulge (December 16, 1944–January 28, 1945). Germany's defeat and the end of Hitler's Third Reich loomed clear.

With his armies in full retreat on all fronts, Hitler abandoned the upper rooms of his chancellery in Berlin and in his final days converted to an underground life in his bunker beneath the chancellery.

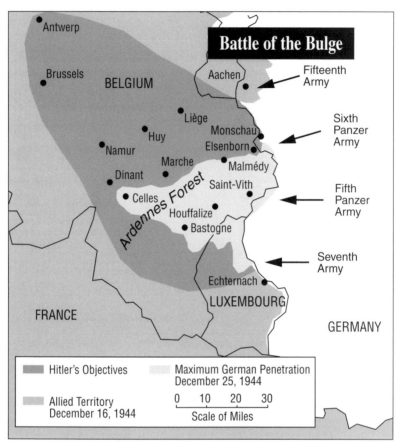

Battle of the Bulge

Antwerp

Brussels

BELGIUM

Aachen

Fifteenth
Army

Liège

Huy

Monschau

Namur

Elsenborn

Sixth
Panzer
Army

Marche

Malmédy

Dinant

Ardennes Forest

Saint-Vith

Celles

Fifth
Panzer
Army

Houffalize

Bastogne

Seventh
Army

Echternach

LUXEMBOURG

FRANCE

GERMANY

Hitler's Objectives

Maximum German Penetration
December 25, 1944

Allied Territory
December 16, 1944

0   10   20   30

Scale of Miles

He claimed that the incessant air raids deprived him of sleep and affected his work. Albert Speer later described how Hitler had at last surrendered his grip on reality:

> The isolation of this bunker world, encased on all sides by concrete and earth, put the final seal on Hitler's separation from the tragedy which was going on outside under the open sky. He no longer had any relationship to it. When he talked about the end, he meant his own and not that of the nation. He had reached the last station in his flight from reality, a reality which he had refused to acknowledge since his youth. At the time I had a name for this unreal world of the bunker: I called it the Isle of the Departed.[28]

When outside bomb bursts sent shock waves rippling through the bunker's sixteen-foot-thick walls, Hitler, a bundle of nerves and no longer able to conceal his reactions, cringed and trembled. Speer wondered what had become of the once-brave corporal of World War I.

In defeat, Hitler rapidly fell to pieces—physically, mentally, and emotionally—but refused to accept the tiniest personal responsibility for Germany's fate. He shunted the blame for his failures off on the Wehrmacht, his officer corps, his civil administrators, the German people themselves, and, most of all, the Jews. Nearing his own end, Hitler directed Albert Speer to carry out a "scorched earth" policy throughout Germany.

Hitler's instructions called for the destruction of not only war production plants and matériel, but also of all the essential elements of life and social order: food and medical supplies, public utilities,

---

Last Visit

Adolf Hitler spent his final days, from April 20 to April 30, 1945, in the *Führerbunker* (Leader's Bunker) beneath the Reich Chancellery and its garden. In *Inside the Third Reich*, Albert Speer describes his last visit to the bunker:

> It was about three o'clock in the morning. Hitler was awake again. I sent word that I wanted to bid him good-by. The day had worn me out, and I was afraid that I would not be able to control myself at our parting. Trembling, the prematurely aged man stood before me for the last time; the man to whom I had dedicated my life twelve years before. I was both moved and confused. For his part, he showed no emotion when we confronted one another. His words were as cold as his hand: "So, you're leaving? Good. *Auf Wiedersehen* (Till we meet again)." No regards to my family, no wishes, no thanks, no farewell. For a moment I lost my composure, said something about coming back. But he could easily see that it was a white lie, and turned his attention to something else. I was dismissed.

The ruins of the bunker where Hitler spent his final days.

When it was clear that Germany had lost the war, Hitler called upon Albert Speer to destroy all means of survival for the German people.

communication centers, bank and public records, and more, including the razing of historical monuments and sites, castles, theaters, and churches. When Speer pointed out that such actions would deny the German people all means of survival, Hitler icily replied:

> If the war is to be lost, the people will be lost also. It is not necessary to worry about what the German people will need for elemental survival. On the contrary, it is best for us to destroy even these things. For the nation has proved to be the weaker, and the future belongs solely to the stronger eastern nation. In any case only those who are inferior will remain after this struggle, for the good have already been killed.[29]

Hitler erred on a grand scale and assigned blame to all but himself. In his last testament, he ascribed blame for his troubles to a variety of reasons, not least of which was his friendship with the Italian dictator Benito Mussolini—*Il Duce.*

Der Führer and *Il Duce:* A Flawed Friendship

Chapter 2

Anything would have been better than having [Italians] as comrades in arms.
— Adolf Hitler, quoted in *Why the Allies Won the War* by Richard Overy

O N OCTOBER 22, 1922, Benito Mussolini marched on Rome and seized power in Italy. Mussolini, who called himself *Il Duce* (The Leader)—just as Hitler would proclaim himself *Der Führer* more than a decade later—bullied the Chamber of Deputies and forced Premier Luigi Facta to resign. Italy's King Emmanuel III appointed Mussolini prime minister a few days later.

Within a year *Il Duce*, the blustery, bombastic son of a blacksmith and a schoolteacher, transformed the Italian democracy (which had been patterned after that of Great Britain) into a dictatorship. He took over the armed forces and directed foreign affairs himself. Suspending civil rights and ruling by decree, Mussolini discouraged political opposition by imprisoning or exiling rival leaders, banning public meetings, suppressing newspapers, establishing strict censorship, firing university professors, and commissioning military tribunals to try all dissenters.

Il Duce's march on Rome did not escape the enterprising eye of Adolf Hitler. He saw in Mussolini's rapid rise an avenue to authority worthy of emulation. In November of the following year, Hitler orchestrated an unsuccessful attempt to overthrow the Bavarian government by force and ended up in jail. Hitler's rise to power, unlike Mussolini's, was to lead him along a crooked path and up a slippery slope. Even so, the careers of both despots bore many similarities, and a decade and a half later the two dictators were to become fast friends. But when their paths first crossed in the summer of 1934, the two tyrants met at loggerheads and narrowly averted a clash of arms.

Mussolini's Bluster Wins the Day

Hitler, an Austrian by birth, had long advocated Germany's annexation of neighboring Austria, not because of what Germany could do for Austria but rather for what Austria could do for Germany. On the first page of *Mein Kampf,* he declared:

> German-Austria must return to the great German mother country, and not because of any economic considerations. No, and again no: even if such a union were unimportant from an economic point of view; yes, even if it were harmful, it must nevertheless take place. One blood demands one Reich.[30]

Upon proclaiming himself Il Duce *in 1922, Mussolini transformed Italy's democracy into a dictatorship.*

To Hitler, the annexation of Austria—that is, the *Anschluss*, or union—represented an early step in achieving living space for Germans. But to Mussolini, a German presence on his northern border posed a threat to Italy's national security. *Il Duce* had expansionist notions of his own and harbored doubts as to whether his ideas were compatible with those of Germany's new dictator, particularly in the context of southeastern Europe.

Mussolini knew that Hitler's plans for assimilating people of German blood into a greater Germany would eventually include Austrians living in the South Tirol—an alpine region that Austria had ceded to Italy by the Treaty of St. Germain in 1919. On March 17, 1934, *Il Duce* concluded a pact with Austria and Hungary that called for closer economic ties and frequent consultations. Although Hitler subsequently promised to leave Austria alone, *Il Duce* did not trust his fellow dictator.

Mussolini's fears seemed justified when Nazi storm troopers dressed in Austrian uniforms attacked the Austrian chancellery and

---

 ## Impressions of Mussolini

In February 1940 U.S. undersecretary of state Sumner Welles met with Benito Mussolini, while on a fact-finding tour in Europe. In the following excerpt from *The War, 1939–1945,* edited by Desmond Flower and James Reeves, the secretary describes his impressions of the Italian dictator:

> My first impression was one of profound astonishment at Mussolini's appearance. In the countless times I had seen him in photographs and in motion pictures and in the many descriptions I had read of him I had always gained the impression of an active, quick-moving, exceedingly animated personality. The man I saw before me seemed fifteen years older than his actual age of fifty-six. He was ponderous and static rather than vital. He moved with an elephantine motion; every step appeared an effort. He was heavy for his height, and his face in repose fell in rolls of flesh. His close-cropped hair was snow-white. During our long and rapid interchange of views he kept his eyes shut a considerable part of the time. He opened them with his dynamic and often-described wide stare only when he desired particularly to underline some remark. At his side was a large cup of some hot brew which he sipped from time to time.
>
> Mussolini impressed me as a man laboring under a tremendous strain. One could almost sense a leaden oppression.

---

assassinated the Austrian chancellor, Engelbert Dollfuss. He hastily mobilized four divisions on the Brenner Pass (which connects Austria with Italy) to guard Austria's independence. Mussolini made a special trip to Vienna to express his outrage over Dollfuss's slaying to Austrian vice chancellor Prince Ernst Rüdiger von Starhemberg:

> It would mean the end of European civilization if [Germany] were to overrun Europe. . . . Hitler is the murderer of Dollfuss, Hitler is the guilty man, he is responsible for this. . . . [Hitler] is a horrible sexual degenerate, a dangerous fool. [And Nazism is] a revolution of the old Germanic tribes in the primeval forest against the Latin civilization of Rome.

In his clipped, repetitive style of oratory, *Il Duce* went on to deny the similarities between Nazism and his own political philosophy, fascism:

> Fascism is a regime that is rooted in the great cultural tradition of the Italian people; Fascism recognizes the right of the individual, it recognizes religion and family. National Socialism, on the other hand, is savage barbarism; in common with barbarian hordes it allows no rights to the individual; the chieftain is lord over life and death of his people. Murder and killing, loot and pillage and blackmail are all it can produce.[31]

Rather than risk a premature military encounter with the fascist leader, Hitler quickly backed off his plans for an immediate *Anschluss* in Austria, content for the moment to preach peace and to quietly proceed with German rearmament. He would wait and watch for a better time. Mussolini's bluster had won the day with Hitler—at least for the moment.

Brutal Alliance

Despite the confrontational beginning to their relationship, Hitler recognized the need to win the support of Mussolini's Italy, which, because of its totalitarian regime, he considered a natural ally. He had only to wait a year and allow unfolding events to determine his next move.

On October 3, 1935, to the indignation of most of the civilized world, Mussolini began his invasion of Ethiopia, then known as Abyssinia. The League of Nations—an international organization formed after World War I to promote world peace and security—responded by imposing limited sanctions on Italy. The sanctions were not only limited, but only partially enforced. Moreover, prohibited exports purposely did not include oil or other commodities that might provoke Mussolini into fighting a war. Hitler came away the big winner in the crisis, as correspondent William L. Shirer noted in his diary on October 4, 1935:

> The Wilhelmstrasse [that is, Hitler] is delighted. Either Mussolini will stumble and get himself so heavily involved in Africa that he will be greatly weakened in Europe, whereupon Hitler can seize Austria, hitherto protected by the Duce; or he will win, defying Britain and France, and thereupon be ripe for a tie-up with Hitler against the Western democracies. Either way Hitler wins.[32]

The flow of events soon validated Shirer's observation. While Europe and the world chorused its disapproval—but did not act—Hitler refused to join in the world's condemnation of Italy and thereby won Mussolini's gratitude. Mussolini began rethinking his relationship with Hitler and the Nazis and softening his rhetoric toward them.

Italian soldiers carry a bust of Mussolini through the streets of Addis Ababa after Italy's forceful acquisition of Ethiopia in 1936.

On May 2, 1936, Italian troops entered Addis Ababa, the Ethiopian capital. A week later Mussolini announced his great victory to 400,000 cheering admirers in Rome's Piazza Venezia. *Il Duce* had delivered his long-promised living space and taken his first step toward building a new Roman empire. His demonstration of land acquisition by force did not go unnoticed in Berlin.

Hitler and Mussolini drew closer together two months later. On July 16 General Francisco Franco staged an armed revolt in Spain, touching off a civil war. Both dictators joined in sending Franco military aid. Their common cause in Spain opened the door to an alliance known as the Rome-Berlin Axis, a joint policy for Germany and Italy agreed to in Berlin on October 21 and publicly announced in Rome by Mussolini on November 1. *Il Duce* referred to the alignment of Italy and Germany as an "Axis," around which the other European nations "may work together."[33] The term was soon to become infamous, and the brutal alliance between the two nations would ultimately destroy them both.

Recurring Behavior

On March 13, 1938, Hitler at last concluded his long-desired union with Austria—the *Anschluss*—this time with Mussolini in his Axis camp. Hitler informed Mussolini in advance of the impending annexation. Mussolini—who was still pledged to defend Austria—elected not to interfere. An enormously grateful Hitler vowed never to forget Mussolini's decision: "I will never forget, whatever may happen. If he should ever need any help or be in any danger, he can be convinced that I shall stick to him, whatever may happen, even if the whole world were against him."[34]

Hitler and Mussolini further strengthened their relationship at the Munich Conference in the fall. On September 29 Mussolini offered what was supposedly an Italian solution to Hitler's claims against Czechoslovakia, a proposal that had actually been drafted in Berlin and reworked in Rome. But Western negotiators, anxious to appease Hitler, failed to recognize the similarities between Mussolini's proposal and Hitler's earlier demands. They accepted the proposal almost as offered, clearing the way for Germany's annexation of the Sudetenland and cementing the Rome-Berlin partnership.

Axis leaders Hitler and Mussolini are seen here during one of Hitler's trips to Italy.

On May 22, 1939, the two dictators reaffirmed the Rome-Berlin Axis, agreeing to the so-called Pact of Steel, which pledged mutual military assistance. In the years ahead, Hitler would honor his pledges to *Il Duce* on countless occasions, doubtlessly expecting a reciprocal commitment from Mussolini. But Mussolini would let him down with regularity. In so doing, he would become a major contributor to the collapse of the European Axis.

Il Duce's first breach of faith came only a week before Hitler's armies crossed into Poland, a time when Hitler surely expected solidarity from his Axis partner. Mussolini had reluctantly accepted Hitler's political accommodation with Stalin on August 23 (Hitler-Stalin Pact), but two days later reneged on his Pact of Steel promises. The Italian armed forces, despite their Abyssinian victory and participation in the war in Spain, were ill-equipped and unprepared for a full-scale war. On August 25, 1939, in a letter to Hitler, a humbled *Il Duce* wrote:

> This is one of the most painful moments of my life, but I must tell you that Italy is not ready for war. My chiefs of staff advise me that our fuel reserves would last only for three weeks. Please understand my position.[35]

Hitler understood. "The Italians are behaving just as they did in 1914," he said. And the chancellery halls and chambers echoed that evening with harsh harangues about the "disloyal Axis partner."[36]

Junior Partner

Despite what he saw as Mussolini's display of cowardice, Hitler stayed true to his end of their bargain, offering his partner another chance to enter the war. On March 10, with the war going well for Germany, Hitler wrote a letter to Mussolini, encouraging him to join the action: "Duce, all is forgiven. I understand why you could not go to war. But now it is time to share in the fight so that you can share in the spoils."[37] In a meeting at the Brenner Pass a week later, Hitler pushed harder. If Italy wanted dominance over the Mediterranean, he told the granite-chinned *Duce*, Italy must join the fight against Britain and France. Mussolini reluctantly agreed to a limited joint attack in southern France.

On June 10, four days before the fall of Paris, Italy declared war on Britain and France. Eight days later Italian troops commanded by Crown Prince Umberto launched an attack in the south of France, which promptly turned into a fiasco. Umberto's offensive got stuck in the mountains and stopped at the small Riviera town of Menton, managing only to deflate the myth of Italian military might. Mussolini, who had begun his association with Hitler as the dominant figure in the Axis alliance, was now obliged to accept the subordinate role of junior partner.

Crown Prince Umberto led Italy's failed attack in the south of France.

Fortunes

In an effort to reconstitute some of his diminished stature, Mussolini next launched offensives against both Egypt and Greece in the fall of 1940. In late summer of the year, he sensed that final victory lay close at Hitler's hand. Seeking to assure his fair share of the victor's spoils, he told a staff member, "I need a few thousand dead." [38] To that end, and to the greater goal of staking claim to the Suez Canal, he ordered his Libya-based army—some 200,000 strong, commanded by Marshal Rodolfo Graziani—to strike out across the desert into Egypt. "Attack!" exhorted *Il Duce*. "Bring me Cairo." [39]

Graziani attacked on September 13, but British forces checked his advance at Sidi Barrâni, fifty miles inside Egypt, with hundreds of miles still separating him from Suez. By mid-December the British had succeeded in ousting the Italians from Egypt and were preparing to take the offensive in Libya. Graziani had failed to bring Cairo to Mussolini. He had instead brought only more humiliation and another ringing Italian defeat.

As a result of the inability of the Italians to prevail over the British in North Africa, Hitler was forced to come to Mussolini's aid in the desert. He ordered the creation of a special desert tank division and named Field Marshal Erwin Rommel as its commander. It arrived in Libya in March 1941 and soon began carving out a fearsome reputation as the vaunted Afrika Korps.

Meanwhile, Mussolini sent troops into northwest Greece on October 28, 1940, much to the consternation of his senior partner. Hitler feared that Italy's military deficiencies might require him to send German troops to aid his ally at a time when he was already making plans to invade the Soviet Union. Hitler's worst fears materialized when Greek patriots rose up against *Il Duce*'s legions and forced them back across the border into Italian-occupied Albania. There the inept Italians floundered until the Germans bailed them out in the spring of 1941.

Hitler's intervention on behalf of his bumbling Axis soulmate constituted an ongoing drain on Germany's armed forces and resources. His loyalty to Mussolini cost the Germans several hundred thousand casualties and the loss of millions of tons of equipment in Greece, North Africa, Sicily, and Italy. Even after Italian king Victor

German field marshall Erwin Rommel peers out of an armored car during the African campaign.

Fate of a Dictator

On April 25, 1945, Mussolini, then ruling the Italian Social Republic—a puppet state established by Hitler in northern Italy after *Il Duce*'s unseating—attempted to flee across the Italo-Swiss border ahead of the advancing Allied armies. In *Triumph and Tragedy*, Winston Churchill recounts how his flight failed:

> In the evening, followed by a convoy of thirty vehicles containing most of the surviving leaders of Italian Fascism, he drove to the prefecture at Como. He had no coherent plan, and as discussion became useless it was each man for himself. Accompanied by a handful of supporters he attached himself to a small German convoy heading towards the Swiss frontier. The commander of the column was not anxious for trouble with Italian Partisans (guerrillas). The Duce was persuaded to put on a German greatcoat and helmet. But the little party was stopped by Partisan patrols; Mussolini was recognized and taken into custody. Other members, including his mistress Signorina Petacci, were also arrested. On Communist instructions the Duce and his mistress were taken out in a car next day and shot. Their bodies, together with others, were sent to Milan and strung up head downward on meat hooks in a petrol [gas] station on the Piazzale Loreto, where a group of Italian Partisans had lately been shot in public. . . .

Such was the fate of the Italian dictator.

Emmanuel III—with the support of the army high command and fascist leaders—deposed Mussolini in July 1943, the continuing Italian campaign tied down some sixteen to twenty Wehrmacht divisions. From a German perspective, they might have been better deployed on the Eastern Front or at Normandy. In a military sense, with friends like *Il Duce*, Hitler needed few enemies.

Mussolini's military gaffe in Greece caused Hitler to postpone the launch of Operation Barbarossa—the invasion of the Soviet Union—from mid-May to late June. Had it not been for the loss of several weeks of dry weather at the start of Barbarossa, German troops might well have marched triumphantly into Moscow before the onset of the Russian winter. Instead, they slogged to an icy stop within sight of the Kremlin's towers. Such are the vicissitudes of war; such were the fortunes of a flawed friendship.

Barbarossa: War on Two Fronts

Chapter 3

So long as war in the West was undecided, any new undertaking must result in war on two fronts, and Adolf Hitler's Germany was even less capable of fighting such a war than had been the Germany of 1914.

—General Heinz Guderian, chief of the high command
of the German army, quoted in *War in Europe*
by Sidney C. Moody Jr. and the Associated Press

ARMCHAIR GENERALS HAVE scratched their heads in puzzlement for more than half a century, questioning why Hitler opened his war against Russia in June 1941, while still struggling with a determined British antagonist in the west. Over the previous summer and fall, Hitler's Luftwaffe had lost the Battle of Britain, partly because of a twist in fate and partly because of Hitler's own interference with the Luftwaffe's attack strategy.

When a few Luftwaffe bombers strayed off course and mistakenly bombed London rather than the oil docks at nearby Thameshaven, British prime minister Winston Churchill ordered instant reprisal raids on Berlin. An irate Hitler retaliated. "If they attack our cities, we will raze *theirs* to the ground," he raged. "We will stop the handiwork of these air pirates, so help us God." [40]

Hitler then ordered Luftwaffe commander Hermann Göring to shift the targets of his bombing offensive over Britain from fighter air stations and aircraft manufacturing plants to London and other cities. Had he gone for a knockout of the fighter stations and manufacturing plants, Hitler might have won not only the Battle of Britain but also a

Difficult Questions

Luftwaffe fighter general Adolf Galland never once conceded defeat in the Battle of Britain, only that Hitler had left it undecided. In his World War II memoir, *The First and the Last*, Galland speculates:

> What would have happened had Hitler not attacked Russia and had he used the pause in the Battle of Britain enforced by the weather to replenish and restrengthen his Luftwaffe, in order to end the interrupted struggle, which so far no one had won? What would have happened had the Battle of Britain been started immediately after the fall of France instead of only in July, whereby the Luftwaffe would have gained four or six weeks before the start of the unfavorable autumn weather? What would have happened had the Sea Lion—whose expected jump had been awaited in all seriousness by the English war leaders—not been recalled by Hitler? Could the English forces have withstood the German onslaught? Even today these questions are still difficult to answer.

victory over England itself and an early end to World War II. His ill-advised decision to switch bombing targets likely cost him a battle. Hitler's next decision—the invasion of the Soviet Union—would arguably cost him the war.

Master of Deception

Despite his struggle with Britain, Hitler had never held the slightest doubt that the Soviet Union represented Germany's foremost enemy. Lest anyone doubt his designs on the eastern territories, in *Mein Kampf* Hitler asserts:

> If we speak of soil in Europe today, we primarily have in mind only *Russia* and her vassal border states. . . . The [giant] empire in the east is ripe for collapse. And the end of Jewish rule in Russia will also be the end of Russia as a state.[41]

A decade later, in a 1934 conversation with the then Nazi politician Hermann Rauschning, Hitler confided:

> We cannot in any way evade the final battle between German race ideals and pan-Slav mass ideals. Here yawns the eternal abyss which no political interest can bridge. We alone can conquer the great continental space, and it will be done singly and alone.[42]

However, Hitler had also long believed that the Soviets could be attacked and conquered only after the defeat of the Western powers. Nonetheless, with the battle still raging with Britain, he inexplicably persuaded himself that the Soviet Union had somehow grown more vulnerable than before, when in reality nothing had happened to alter the strategic situation in the east.

Hitler now saw himself as the *Grofaz—Grosster Fedheer Allen Zeiten*, or greatest military commander of all time. His inflated thinking led him to conclude that he had only to unleash the Nazi war machine in the east, quickly crush the Soviets, then turn the full force of his arms and resources against the British, whom he could then finish off handily. As later events would illustrate, Hitler proved more adept at the art of deception than at the art of war.

Hitler had initiated the planning for the attack on the Soviet Union in June 1940, while his panzers were still closing in on Paris. He assigned the details to Colonel Bernhard von Lossberg, who drafted a thirty-page outline and named it *Fall Fritz* (Case Fritz) after his son. Then the OKW massaged and tweaked the plan and submitted it to the führer for approval. Chief of operations General Alfred Jodl, one of Hitler's toadies, encouraged Hitler to go ahead with the attack, commenting, "The Russian colossus will prove to be a pig's bladder. Prick it and it will burst." [43]

Hitler renamed the plan Case Barbarossa (anglicized as Operation Barbarossa). On December 18, 1940, he signed his historic Directive 21. Its sinister beginning left no doubt as to Hitler's intent: "The German Armed Forces must be prepared to crush Soviet Russia in a quick campaign even before the conclusion of the war with England. The directive went on to set May 15, 1941, as the completion date for all preparations. It also cautioned, "It is to be considered of decisive importance . . . that the intention to attack is not discovered." [44]

As a ploy to divert Stalin's attention from his real aims, Hitler had already invited the Soviet dictator to join the Tripartite Pact, signed by Germany, Italy, and Japan on September 27, 1940. Stalin declined to join the pact, but he never suspected that Hitler was preparing to attack him.

Because unanticipated problems in the Balkans forced Hitler's intervention—Mussolini's fiasco in Greece; delays in persuading Romania, Hungary, and Bulgaria to join the Axis alliance; and partisan guerrilla activities in Yugoslavia—the launch date for Barbarossa was set back by about five weeks.

When the German blitzkrieg roared into the Soviet Union at 3:30 A.M. on June 22, 1941, it achieved total surprise. Nothing better illustrates the shocking effect of the German attack than one Soviet commander's plea to his headquarters: "We are being fired upon; what shall we do?"[45] Masquerading as a friend under the Hitler-Stalin Pact, Hitler surely qualified as a master of deception.

The *Grofaz* Speaks

The German buildup along the Soviet frontier represented the largest arsenal ever assembled in the history of human warfare—153 divisions (3 million men), including 19 panzer divisions with 3,580 tanks, 7,184 cannon, 600,000 motorized vehicles, 625,000 horses, and 2,740 aircraft deployed in the rear. This massive German force was reinforced by 35.5 satellite divisions: 12 Romanian, 18 Finnish, 3 Hungarian, and 2.5 Slovak, joined later by 3 Italian divisions and 1 Spanish division. Hitler truly did not exaggerate when he said, "When Barbarossa commences the world will hold its breath and make no comment!"[46]

German infantrymen advance on Leningrad during Operation Barbarossa.

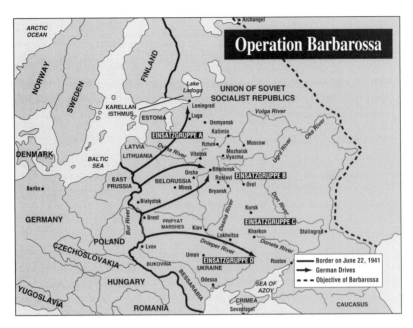

Stalin had received numerous warnings of an impending German attack, through espionage and diplomatic channels, but the Soviets dismissed, even ridiculed, the warnings. The official Soviet news agency TASS declared flatly that rumors of an impending German attack were "completely without foundation." Stalin possibly thought that the huge troop buildup along his borders represented no more than a German ploy to mask Hitler's real plan: the invasion of England. And Soviet foreign minister Molotov scoffed, "Only a fool would attack us."[47] He was right, as time would show, but 3 million "fools" rushed in anyway.

Attacking simultaneously along a 2,000-mile front, from the Barents Sea in the north to the Black Sea in the south, Hitler's forces smashed across the Soviet frontier and roared into Russia in the last German blitzkrieg of the war. Some German units raced fifty miles deep into Russia before the day ended. Behind the Soviet lines, German dive-bombers struck more than sixty enemy airfields and destroyed more than two thousand Soviet aircraft in the first two days.

Facing the Germans along the Western Front, Soviet troops numbered about 3 million with another million scattered elsewhere. Reserves were in great supply. Matériel—tanks, artillery, and planes—was plentiful but of inferior quality to that of the Germans.

Troubling Terrain

The harsh Russian terrain proved rough going for German tanks and vehicles, as can be seen in the following excerpt from *The War, 1939–1945*, edited by Desmond Flower and James Reeves. In "German Difficulties," General Gunther von Blumentritt, German Fourth Army chief of staff, writes:

> It was appallingly difficult country for tank movement—great virgin forests, widespread swamps, terrible roads, and bridges not strong enough to bear the weight of tanks. The resistance also became stiffer, and the Russians began to cover their front with minefields; it was easier for them to block the way because there were so few roads. . . .
>
> Such country was bad enough for the tanks, but worse still for the transport accompanying them—carrying their fuel, their supplies, and all the auxiliary troops they needed. Nearly all this transport consisted of wheeled vehicles, which could not move off the roads, nor move on it if the sand turned into mud. An hour or two of rain reduced the Panzer forces to stagnation. It was an extraordinary sight, with groups of them strung out over a hundred miles stretch, all stuck—until the sun came out and the ground dried.

The superiority of the Germans' war-making machine turned the tide in Hitler's favor—at least initially. By mid-July General Heinz Guderian's Second Panzer Group had captured a half million Soviet prisoners in its drive on Smolensk. When that city fell to forces under General Field Marshal Fedor von Bock, another 300,000 Soviets were taken prisoner. Few military experts expected the war in the east to last beyond the summer. Hitler himself had predicted, "We have only to kick in the door [to Russia] and the whole rotten structure will come crashing down."[48]

The first three months of Barbarossa seemed to bear out all of Hitler's predictions. In the far north, Baron Carl Gustaf von Mannerheim's Finnish forces reclaimed all of the Finnish lands seized by the Soviets in the Russo-Finnish War, which was fought during the winter of 1939–40. Mannerheim then secured Finland's border and stood in place, reducing the German front to about a thousand miles, extending from the Baltic to the Black Sea.

General Field Marshal Wilhelm Ritter von Leeb's Army Group North advanced toward Leningrad and besieged the city in early October. Kiev, under attack from General Field Marshal Gerd von Rundstedt's Army Group South, capitulated on September 16, and a half million more Russians surrendered.

Despite the apparent success of the German campaign under his subordinates' command, Hitler next took a personal hand in operations. After the fall of Smolensk, he reassigned two panzer groups and an army away from Bock's Army Group Center (including Guderian's Second Panzer Group) and sent them to support Rundstedt's slower-moving Army Group South. Then, during a short lull in mid-August, when his general staff projected plans for continuing the offensive, Hitler complained that their plans were "not in line with my intentions."[49] What followed would prove crucial to the Germans' campaign against the Soviets.

Hitler overruled his generals' proposal to drive on Moscow, which he had earlier insisted upon, and redirected the principal German objectives southward to the Crimea, the industrial Donets River Basin, and the oil-rich Caucasus. His change in strategy left his field generals aghast. Guderian, for one, flew to Hitler's headquarters to

Field Marshall Baron Mannerheim (left) studies a tactical map as his troops prepare to face the Soviets.

*General Heinz Guderian
tried unsuccessfully to
convince Hitler to drive on
Moscow.*

speak on their behalf and urge him to reinstate the plan to drive directly on Moscow.

Guderian was unable to move Hitler or the members of the high command. Hitler listened attentively to Guderian, then, tapping on a wall map, he expounded on the industry, agriculture, and natural resources of the southlands and their potential benefits to Germany. "My generals know nothing about the economic aspects of war," he concluded. Guderian later explained to his senior staff officers that he could do nothing. "I was faced by a solid front of the High Command," he said. "All those present nodded at every sentence the Führer said."[50]

Hitler had spoken and his "yes men" had concurred. It fell not within the province of field generals to fault the decisions of the all-knowing *Grofaz.* Yet, Hitler's mercurial nature meant that no decision was final.

Of Elephants and Ants

On September 6 Hitler changed his mind again. Moscow again became the major objective. The führer's fluctuations and demands placed heavy, frequently impossible, loads on the German war machine. If Hitler had concentrated on one goal and coordinated strategy with his field commanders, he might have knocked the Soviets out of the war in the fall of 1941. But he did not. And to exacerbate his battlefield blunders, Hitler committed the worst offense that a military commander can make: he underestimated his enemy. But he had plenty of company among his generals. "We misjudged the combat strength and combat efficiency of the enemy as well as our own troops,"[51] General Hans von Grieffenberg, Bock's chief of staff, later confessed.

The Soviets—both male and female—fought with uncommon ferocity and tenacity, willing to sacrifice ten Russian lives for one German. General Franz Halder, chief of the German General Staff, observed: "At the beginning we reckoned with some 200 enemy divisions. We have already identified 360. When a dozen of them are destroyed, the Russians throw in another dozen."[52]

The Germans also failed to reckon with the cruel vastness of Russia itself, the characteristics of which the Soviets utilized to their maximum advantage. Soviet strategy generally called for their forces to fall back in the face of the German advance, counterattack intermittently and unpredictably, then fall back again. In this fashion, they drew the Germans deeper and deeper into the haunting barrenness of their vast dominion. While the Germans stretched their lines of communications and supply farther and farther, the Russians played the waiting game. And the calendar edged closer to the delaying rains

A German soldier on the front line lobs a hand grenade during the 1941 Nazi offensive in Russia.

and mud of autumn—and, none too soon for the Soviets, the re-
deeming snows and bitter temperatures of the Russian winter.

Some German military leaders saw disaster looming. German
commander Colonel Bernd von Kleist foretold the German army's
fate in Russia, likening the Wehrmacht to an elephant attacking a
horde of ants: "The elephant will kill thousands, perhaps even millions of ants, but in the end their numbers will overcome him, and he
will be eaten to the bone."[53] And so the behemoth fell.

The Führer Wasn't Listening

In addition to Soviet determination and strategy, logistical problems
beset the Germans. Roads were few and of poor quality, and the Soviet railroad tracks were of a different gauge from the Germans',
making it difficult to move supplies toward the front. And then there
was the weather. The rains started in September, turning the few
roads into quagmires and rendering open spaces impassable. Tanks
and motorized vehicles bogged down in the mire. Supplies dwindled.
Based on Hitler's prediction of a quick victory, panzer divisions had
started the invasion with a month's reserve of diesel fuel. Each
panzer division needed three hundred tons of supplies a day to operate. On a good day, because of 300-mile-long supply lines and prim-
itive railways that had to be converted to German gauge, each
received only seventy tons. The Germans' lightning advance slowed
to a crawl.

On October 2 Bock's Army Group Center launched Operation
Typhoon—the final drive on Moscow—with fourteen panzer divisions and three infantry armies. The first snow fell two days later, a
portent of the earliest and severest Russian winter in half a century.
A thaw followed, then a freeze. Temperatures plunged to minus thirty
degrees Celsius (minus twenty-two degrees Fahrenheit). Frostbite
and typhus crippled German soldiers still in summer garb and ill-
equipped for snow and cold. The diesel engines in the German tanks
became balky. Tankers had to light and burn fires for as long as four
hours beneath their machines in order to start them.

Despite their difficulties, Bock's troops drew within sight of the
Kremlin's spires on October 19. Their advance stopped there. That
same day, Stalin addressed the Russian people and touched their
hearts: "The German invaders want a war of extermination against

the peoples of the Soviet Union. Very well then! If they want a war of extermination they shall have it! Our cause is just. Victory will be ours!"[54] To back up his words, Stalin rushed eighteen divisions from his Far Eastern Command by rail to defend Moscow and appointed Marshal Georgy Zhukov to command them.

Moscow remained under siege for several weeks. Then, on December 6 Soviet cannon thundered and glowed red and Zhukov lashed out at the invaders with a fury seldom seen in war. One aghast OKW officer, whose forces bore the brunt of Zhukov's hammering assault, recalled:

> From the depths of Russia, undreamed-of masses of humanity were hurled against us. . . . I can still see the situation maps of the next days and weeks: where until now the blue of our own forces had dominated the picture, with the enemies' red only sparsely sketched in, now from Leningrad right down to the Sea of Azov thick red arrows had sprung up on every sector of the front, pointing at the heart of Germany.[55]

Hitler ordered the Wehrmacht to hold fast. But weary German soldiers, unable to dig in the frozen earth to establish defensive emplacements, fell back along the front, in some places as far as 175 miles from Moscow. The Soviets suffered huge losses—about 3 million casualties between July and November—but the Red Army fought on.

Operation Barbarossa had failed, and the perception of the invincibility of the Wehrmacht had been shattered. By January 31, 1942, German losses—wounded, captured, missing, and dead—totaled 918,000 men, or 28.7 percent of the 3.2 million soldiers who took part in the action. The Wehrmacht never recovered from this decisive defeat—and the Nazi dream began to fade.

Before Hitler launched Barbarossa, propaganda minister Joseph Goebbels had commented, "Germany has never had luck in a two-front war. It won't be able to stand this one in the long run, either."[56] But his führer wasn't listening.

The Holocaust: A Despicable Diversion

Chapter 4

If, with the help of his Marxist creed, the Jew is victorious over the other peoples of the world, his crown will be the funeral wreath of humanity and this planet will, as it did millions of years ago, move through the ether devoid of men.

—Adolf Hitler, *Mein Kampf*

PERHAPS HITLER FAILED TO hear Joseph Goebbels's prophetic forebodings about a two-front war because of a preoccupation with the second vital element of the Nazi dream. Hitler had recognized that the invasion of the Soviet Union would provide him with a vast arena in which to prosecute his campaign against the Jews—a war within a war. Also, with a full-blown shooting war raging in the east, he could shroud his despicable internal activities from external outrage and interference. In short, with the world's attention directed elsewhere, he would be free to kill Jews.

Exactly how much Hitler's campaign against the Jews contributed to Germany's defeat in World War II will likely never be known. But the vast numbers of troops and huge quantities of resources diverted from the fighting fronts to kill Jews might have been used to turn innumerable German battle losses into victories. And wars are generally won by winning one battle at a time. So fades the dream.

It remains unclear today as to precisely when Hitler decided to physically exterminate the Jews of Europe, but actual planning for what the world knows now as the Holocaust began at least as early as July 31, 1941. On that date, Reich Marshal Hermann Göring, next

56

in line to Hitler himself, sent a directive to Reinhard Heydrich, head of the Reich Central Security Office (RSHA):

> In completion of the task which was entrusted to you in the Edict dated January 24, 1939, of solving the Jewish question by means of emigration or evacuation in the most convenient way possible, given the present conditions [the ongoing war with the Soviet Union], I herewith charge you with making all necessary preparations with regard to organizational, practical, and financial aspects for an overall solution [*Gesammtlösung*] of the Jewish question in the German sphere of influence in Europe. I further charge you with submitting to me promptly an overall plan of the preliminary organizational, practical, and financial measures for the execution of the intended final solution [*Endlösung*] of the Jewish question.[57]

As Hitler's deputy, Hermann Göring put into action Hitler's campaign against the Jews.

Göring's use of the phrases "overall solution" and "final solution" clearly suggests that Hitler had reached a firm decision by the end of July 1941. He would now, it seems, exploit the eastern territories to solve the Jewish problem in a way commensurate with his early rantings in *Mein Kampf.*

Hitler's War Against the Jews

Hitler's campaign to eliminate European Jewry—at least from Germany proper—essentially began with the passage of the Enabling Act in Berlin on March 24, 1933, which provided the constitutional foundation for Hitler's dictatorship. Immediately after its passage, Hitler began a program to purge the Third Reich of Jewish influence.

The Final Solution

On January 20, 1942, Reinhard Heydrich, head of the Reich Central Security Office, convened a meeting of fifteen leading Nazi bureaucrats in the Berlin suburb of Grossen-Wannsee to contemplate the extermination of the Jews. He asked the attendees to cooperate "in the implementation of the solution." In this passage taken from Martin Gilbert's *The Holocaust,* Heydrich outlines in chillingly bureaucratic language the first steps of the Final Solution:

Reinhard Heydrich was one of the men charged with implementing Hitler's Final Solution.

> In the course of the final solution, the Jews should be brought under appropriate direction in a suitable manner to the East for labor utilization. Separated by sex, the Jews capable of work will be led into these areas in large labor columns to build roads, whereby doubtless a large part will fall away through natural reduction [death].

> The inevitable final remainder which doubtless constitutes the toughest element will have to be dealt with appropriately [killed], since it represents a natural selection which upon liberation is to be regarded as a germ cell of a new Jewish development.

On September 15, 1935, during the Nazi Party rallies at Nuremberg, a special session of the Reichstag enacted two racial laws that provided the driving force behind Hitler's racist agenda. The first law, *Reichsbürgergesetz*, or Reich Citizenship Law, distinguished between German citizens and subjects; it declared German Jews to be subjects of the German state and thus not entitled to full political rights. The second law, *Gesetz sum Schutze des deutschen Blutes und des deutschen Ehre*, or Law for the Protection of German Blood and Honor, defined who was a Jew, who was an Aryan, and who was a *Mischling*, or part Jew; it prohibited marriage and sexual relations between Germans and Jews. Both laws formed the basis for all subsequent anti-Semitic legislation enacted in Germany and elsewhere in Nazi-controlled Europe.

In introducing the laws to the Reichstag at Nuremberg, Hitler hinted at an ominous future change to his anti-Jewish policy. He described the "Blood and Honor" law as "an attempt to regulate by law a problem that, in the event of repeated failure, would have to be transferred by law to the National Socialist Party for final solution."[58] The phrase "final solution" later became the Nazi euphemism for what the world knows today as the Holocaust—the extermination of nearly 6 million Jews by the Germans during World War II.

The Germans implemented *Die Endlösung*, or the "Final Solution," under the umbrella of *Gleichschaltung*, or cooperation, a Nazi concept dedicated to unifying all aspects of German life and culture in a racially pure Aryan community. This so-called *Neuordnung* (New Order) promised to bring prosperity and worldwide recognition to the German people, and a rebirth of the Teutonic culture.

In Hitler's view, a prerequisite to the New Order's success entailed the culling out and elimination of impure or alien elements:

> *There is only one holiest human right, and this right is at the same time the holiest obligation, to wit: to see to it that the blood is preserved pure and, by preserving the best humanity, to create the possibility of a nobler development of these beings.*[59] (Italics in original.)

The impurities, according to Hitler, were primarily Jews, but also included Slavs, Gypsies, blacks, and others who were not Aryan.

Beginning in 1933, the Nazis gradually drove Jews from public life and reduced them to the status of second-class citizens. The

Nazi soldiers herd Jews from trucks onto trains headed for work camps.

abominable process of ultimate elimination started with exclusion, moved next to persecution, then to expulsion, and finally to annihilation. To oversee and carry out all phases of his Jewish policies, Hitler called on Heinrich Himmler—a former fertilizer salesman, failed chicken rancher, and early Nazi activist—and his SS forces.

Himmler's SS (an acronym for *Schutzstaffel*, or defense echelon) was an elite guard that initially served as political police. This politicized army was assigned the task of administering concentration, labor, and extermination camps. It followed naturally that Hitler should entrust the annihilation phase of his solution to the Jewish "problem" to Reichsführer-SS (Reich leader of the SS) Himmler and what amounted to a band of black-uniformed hoodlums. Himmler vowed, "The SS will be the imperial guard of the new Germany."[60] He might have added that they would also become Hitler's exterminators.

On March 13, 1941, Field Marshal Wilhelm Keitel, chief of the German high command, issued five copies of a top-secret directive applicable to the impending invasion of the Soviet Union. The directive defined the roles, authority, and operational areas assigned to the armed forces, the SS, and the civil administration (of conquered territories). One paragraph of the directive read, in part:

In the area of army operations the Reichsführer-SS [Himmler] will be entrusted, on behalf of the Führer, with *special tasks* for the preparation of the *political administration*—tasks entailed by the final struggle that will have to be carried out between two opposing political systems [Nazism and communism]. Within the framework of these tasks, the Reichsführer-SS will act independently and on his own responsibility.[61]

A Foot in the Door

Next to Hitler himself, Reichsführer-SS Heinrich Himmler arguably became the most powerful man in Nazi Germany. His influence extended even to industry and top-secret programs. In *Inside the Third Reich*, Albert Speer offers this example:

> After Hitler became excited over the V-2 [rocket] project, Himmler entered the picture. Six weeks later he came to Hitler to propose the simplest way to guarantee secrecy for this vital program. If the entire work force were concentration camp prisoners, all contact with the outside world would be eliminated. Such prisoners did not even have any mail, Himmler said. Along with this, he offered to provide all necessary technicians from the ranks of the prisoners. All industry would have to furnish would be the management and the engineers.
>
> Hitler agreed to this plan. . . .
>
> The result was that we had to work out guidelines for a joint undertaking with the SS leadership—what was to be called the Central Works. My assistants went into it reluctantly, and their fears were soon confirmed. Formally speaking, we remained in charge of the manufacturing; but in cases of doubt we had to yield to the superior power of the SS leadership. Thus, Himmler had put a foot in our door, and we ourselves had helped him do it. . . .
>
> Our hard-won independence in matters of armaments was broken by Hitler's order to erect a large rocket-production plant dependent on the SS.

Heinrich Himmler glares at a prisoner at Dachau concentration camp.

Thus did Hitler grant enormous power to the bespectacled SS chief, whose handpicked SS murderers and cutthroats were to operate independently behind the lines. Himmler and his SS would answer only to the führer himself in carrying out the last act of Hitler's war against the Jews.

The Exterminators

Reichsführer-SS Himmler delegated the job of recruiting SS members for the "special tasks" referred to in Field Marshal Keitel's directive to RSHA chief Reinhard Heydrich. Tall and blond, Heydrich displayed the Nordic features that caused Carl Jacob Burckhardt, onetime president of the International Red Cross, to fittingly label him "a young evil god of death."[62]

Heydrich quickly selected three thousand men from a surplus of volunteers and organized them into four *Einsatzgruppen* (task forces), special mobile killing groups designated with the letters A through D. The four *Einsatzgruppen* were further split into subunits called *Sonderkommandos/Einsatzkommandos* (special units/killer units). At the onset of Barbarossa, the *Einsatzgruppen* followed the

Hitler's murderous SS guards stand in formation at the Belzec death camp.

Wehrmacht into the Soviet Union along a thousand-mile front, extending from the Baltic to the Black Sea.

Each task force developed its own killing style. Otto Ohlendorf, commander of *Einsatzgruppe* D, behind the Eleventh Army in the southern sector, described a typical task force operation:

> The unit selected would enter a village or city and order the prominent Jewish citizens to call together all Jews for the purpose of resettlement. They were requested to hand over their valuables and, shortly before execution, to surrender their outer clothing. The men, women, and children were led to a place of execution, which in most cases was located next to a deeply excavated antitank ditch. Then they were shot, kneeling or standing, and the corpses thrown into the ditch.[63]

This procedure was exercised again and again in countless Polish and Soviet villages, towns, and cities by the elite *Einsatzgruppen*—the official exterminators of the Third Reich.

The needs of the Wehrmacht often ran counter to those of the SS, causing friction between them and lowering the efficiency of both organizations. Much needed war matériel went unmanufactured because of a shortage of laborers, while Jews with skills that the Germans might have exploited were being shipped off to death camps for execution. Trains and trucks, railways and roads, and other forms of transport that might have been used to rush troops and goods to the fighting front were diverted to deport Jews to their deaths. SS personnel that might have been used to man frontline ramparts were deployed behind the lines to execute their grisly killing tasks. But Hitler almost always ruled in favor of his SS exterminators when conflicts arose between them and the Wehrmacht, often to the detriment of military strategies.

Babi Yar

As the *Einsatzgruppen* moved across Soviet-occupied eastern Poland, Lithuania, Latvia, Estonia, and the Soviet Union itself behind the advancing German armies, their sole aim was to eliminate Jewish life altogether. Local police and paramilitary groups in these regions joined the Germans in the slaughter of the Jews, as did Romanians in Bessarabia, Moldavia, and parts of southern Russia. One of the worst examples of German killing efficiency occurred outside Kiev, a Ukrainian city 470 miles southwest of Moscow.

On September 16, 1941, elements of the German Sixth Army finally entered the city after hammering at Soviet defenses for forty-five days. A few days later, violent explosions rocked the Continental Hotel and surrounding areas. The hotel was then serving as the headquarters of a German command post. Untold numbers of German soldiers died in a rash of fires that followed the blast. The Germans, perhaps frustrated by their long struggle to conquer Kiev, held the city's Jews responsible for the sizable loss of German lives and sought immediate retribution.

During the two days of September 27 and 28, the Germans assembled more than thirty-three thousand Jews—men, women, children, the very young, and the very old. German soldiers marched them, under guard, along Melnik Street and through the Jewish cemetery to a ravine northwest of the city called Babi Yar. There, at gunpoint, the Jews were ordered to turn over all their valuables and to disrobe. The Germans then herded them to the edge of the ravine in small groups and machine-gunned them to death.

Just after the war, a watchman at the Jewish cemetery—a non-Jew—recalled how Ukrainian policemen (in the service of the Germans)

> formed a corridor and drove the panic-stricken people towards the huge glade, where sticks, swearings, and dogs, who were tearing the people's bodies, forced the people to undress, to form columns in hundreds, and then to go in the columns in twos towards the mouth of the ravine.

> [There, the watchman recalled] . . . they found themselves on the narrow ground above the precipice, twenty to twenty-five meters in height, and on the opposite side there were the Germans' machine guns. The killed, wounded and half-alive people fell down and were smashed there. Then the next hundred were brought, and everything repeated again. The policemen took the children by the legs and threw them alive down into the Yar.

That evening, the watchman testified, the Germans collapsed the wall of the ravine and covered the bodies with thick layers of earth. So great was the number of people buried alive that the earth continued to move long into the night. One girl, crying, asked: "Mammy, why do they pour the sand into my eyes?"[64]

A Better Way to Kill

Hitler's despicable war against the Jews would continue to rage over the next four years. As at Babi Yar, the *Einsatzgruppe* exterminators massacred tens of thousands of Jews in like fashion, shooting down their victims in ditches, gravel pits, ravines, and fields near every village and town in the path of the German advance in the summer and fall of 1941. Five of the worst mass murders took place at Ponar (near Wilno, Lithuania/Belarus), Kaiserwald (near Riga, Latvia), Fort Nine at Kovno (Lithuania), the Drobitsky ravine at Kharkov (Ukraine), and the Ratomskaya ravine at Minsk (Belarus). Nazi exterminators also wiped out large Jewish populations in Kishinev (Moldova) and Odessa (Ukraine).

An order issued on October 10, 1941, by Field Marshal Walther von Reichenau, commander of the German Sixth Army, suggests that the

Two SS guards supervise as Jewish prisoners are forced to dig graves for executed Jews during the Babi Yar massacre.

aims of the campaign in Russia went well beyond Hitler's objectives of gaining *Lebensraum* for the German people: "The main objective of this campaign against the Jewish-Bolshevik system is to totally destroy the potential for power and to extirpate Asiatic influence on European cultural life."[65] The order went on to emphasize the need for measures beyond those normally expected of soldiers and advocated maximum cruelty toward those conquered in order to ensure victory. An enthusiastic Hitler ordered distribution of Reichenau's order to all army units.

By November 1941 the *Einsatzgruppen* had liquidated possibly as many as 600,000 Jews, but the strain of slaughtering masses of human beings began to tell even on the hardened SS assassins. Many of them, unable to endure the bloodletting any longer, resorted to suicide. Others sought relief in alcohol in order to perform their gory tasks. Still others went mad. On one occasion, after witnessing the execution of about a hundred Jews with Heinrich Himmler, *Einsatzgruppe* general Erich von dem Bach-Zelewski told Reichsführer-SS Himmler that these war crimes were ruining the effectiveness of the SS troops: "Look at the eyes of the men in this *Kommando*, how deeply shaken they are! These men are finished for the rest of their lives. What kind of followers are we training here? Either neurotics or savages!"[66] Shortly afterward, Bach-Zelewski himself succumbed to severe stomach and intestinal disorders related to his duties and was hospitalized. Himmler now recognized the need for more efficient methods for mass executions—a better way to kill.

The Führer Gambles

German technocrats quickly devised two new methods for mass murder: gas vans, in which victims were killed by exhaust fumes during transport; and specially designed gas chambers, at permanent camp sites, in which victims were gassed to death with Zyklon B gas. Gas vans proved to be inefficient and too costly for large-scale operations, but gas chambers excelled in meeting the demands of Hitler's Final Solution. The Germans now established six death camps in German-occupied Poland, at Chelmno, Sobibor, Belzec, Treblinka, Birkenau, and Majdanek—sites forever emblazoned in the annals of the world's great atrocities.

As soon as the first death camp became "operational" (Chelmno in December 1941), the Germans started transporting Jews and others

Concentration Camps Throughout Europe

that the Nazis considered subhuman there for extermination. Under the banefully efficient direction of Adolf Eichmann, head of Reich Central Security Office's Section IV B4 for Jewish Affairs, the victims were shipped by rail from all points within the sphere of German influence. According to Rudolf Höss, commandant at Auschwitz-Birkenau, "The solution to the Jewish question was Eichmann's life mission."[67]

In August 1944 Eichmann reported to Himmler that some 4 million Jews had died in the death camps and that another 2 million had been killed by mobile extermination units. From the summer of 1941 until the end of the war in Europe, the killing of Jews went on and on, for their total annihilation kept alive the Nazi illusion of an Aryan master race. Ironically, the Nazi effort to exterminate the Jews and its associated diversion of troops, equipment, and supplies from the fighting fronts became a major contributor to the demise of their dream.

Friction between the SS and the Wehrmacht surfaced as early as December 1941, when the Wehrmacht fell prey to the ravages of the Russian winter during the siege of Moscow. Because of the lack of cold-weather gear and a shortage of military equipment, apparatus, and supplies that the efficient use of skilled Jewish laborers might have made available, the Wehrmacht offensive ground to a halt at the gates of Moscow. Wehrmacht leaders complained that the production of war matériel was vital to the army's success and that qualified Jewish workers should be used in that critical capacity whenever possible. Field commanders elevated the Wehrmacht's complaints against the indiscriminate extermination of Jewish workers to Berlin for resolution. Berlin's terse reply on December 16 clearly established Hitler's

Adolf Eichmann was responsible for the deportation and execution of millions of Jews.

"In Accordance with the Führer's Wishes"

Despite the German labor shortage, Hitler refused to let production needs interfere with the killing of Jews. Lucy S. Dawidowicz, in her acclaimed *The War Against the Jews*, illuminates Hitler's wartime priorities:

> In the Generalgouvernement [Nazi-occupied Poland] the conflict between the army and the SS sharpened after July 19, 1942, when Himmler ordered the "resettlement" of all the Jews in the Generalgouvernement by the end of the year. . . . Of the more than 1 million workers in war industries, over 300,000 were Jews, one-third of them skilled workers. Their immediate removal [asserted General Curt Ludwig Freiherr von Gienanth, commander of the military district of Nazi-occupied Poland] "would cause the Reich's war potential to be considerably reduced and supplies to the front as well as to the troops in the Generalgouvernement to be at least temporarily halted." Gienanth asked that the removal of the Jews be postponed until certain essential war production was completed, since he was prepared to accept the principle that the Jews were to be eliminated "as promptly as possible without impairing essential war work."

> [Himmler issued a blistering response and further instructed] "that steps be ruthlessly taken against all those who think it is their business to intervene [with the extermination of Jews] in the alleged interests of war industry, and who in reality only want to support the Jews and their businesses." (On September 30 Gienanth had been relieved of his command.) The consolidation of Jewish munitions workers into "a few large concentration-camp enterprises" was the next step, but, Himmler concluded, "even from there the Jews are someday to disappear, in accordance with the Führer's wishes."

priority: "As a matter of principle, economic considerations [production of war matériel] should be overlooked in the solution of the problem."[68] The führer wanted it all and gambled to get it. But he lost that gamble, and with that loss the dream faded further.

Although it would be an overstatement to say that the Holocaust caused Germany's defeat, Hitler's despicable diversion surely cost him more than he could afford to lose.

The Clash of
Economies and
Chapter 5 # Technology

*Many battlefields have been cited as being particularly signifi-
cant for Germany's defeat in World War II. Not the least of them
should be Detroit.*
> —John Ellis, quoted in *War in Europe* by Sidney
> C. Moody Jr. and the Associated Press

HE NAZI DREAM FADED further yet in the summer of 1943, when
the Allies started bombing German industrial sites in earnest. By
then, Germany faced the vast combined wartime outputs of three
of the world's four greatest economies—Britain, the Soviet Union, and
the United States (Germany itself ranked second behind the United
States)—but Germany's own industrial output continued to rise steeply
until the summer of 1944. On balance, however, the Allies utilized their
industrial and scientific astuteness better than the Germans, and thus
won the clash of economies and technology.

Between 1942 and 1945, the Allies together *exceeded* German
production figures by 156,000 tanks and self-propelled guns, 4.07
million machine guns, and 400,248 aircraft, including 133,000 fighters, while outproducing the Axis 7 to 1 in steel and 47 to 1 in oil.
Small wonder that noted historian John Ellis concludes, "A Reich
that would wage a blitzkrieg war with only 47,000 tanks versus its
enemy's 227,000, 116,000 guns versus 915,000, and 350,000 trucks
versus 3 million . . . has not much real chance of imposing its will." [69]

Germany's loss on the economic warfare front can again be
traced to Hitler himself. Although the führer thought of himself as an
expert in economics, he either failed or refused to recognize the im-

portance of economic warfare, and thus the concept played little or no role in Axis strategy. True, German submarines prosecuted a stout campaign against Allied shipping during the Battle of the Atlantic, and the German bombing blitz against Britain was partially directed against British ports; but neither campaign formed a part of a greater strategic plan, nor were they coordinated with any agenda calculated to undermine Allied economies.

From an Allied perspective, victory in the economic warfare sector came only as the result of no less than three timely miracles. The first occurred in Britain.

The Beaver Keeps Them Flying

In the summer of 1940, after the Germans' lightning campaign across most of western Europe, Britain stood alone to face the Nazi scourge. Britain endured and eventually prevailed over Hitler's minions because of a variety of circumstances: the spirit and determination of the British people; Hitler's indecisiveness and vacillations, his failure to strike across the Channel at Britain immediately after the fall of France, and his fateful decision to invade the Soviet Union before knocking Britain out of the war; the guts and skills of a handful of blue-clad fighter pilots of the RAF (Royal Air Force); and, to keep them flying, the British aircraft industry.

 ## Slowing Down the Panzers

Because of development and production problems on the home front, German panzer divisions never reached their full potential. In this excerpt from Matthew Cooper's *The German Army, 1933–1945*, panzer general Heinz Guderian tells why:

> The development of tracked vehicles for the tank supporting arms never went as fast as we wished. It was clear that the effectiveness of the tanks would gain in proportion to the ability of the infantry, artillery, and other divisional arms to follow them in an advance across country. We wanted lightly armed half-tracks for the riflemen, combat engineers, and medical services; armored self-propelled guns for the artillery and the anti-tank battalions; and various types of armor for the reconnaissance and signals battalions. The equipment of the divisions with these vehicles was never fully completed.

Britain's aircraft manufacturers at first did not seem up to the job of producing the planes needed to turn back the German air attacks. As a result, one of Winston Churchill's first acts after becoming Britain's prime minister on May 10, 1940, was to put an end to "the muddle and scandal of the (Air Ministry's) aircraft and production branch."[70] To tackle the tough assignment, Churchill appointed sixty-one-year-old Canadian newspaper tycoon William Maxwell Aitken, first Baron Beaverbrook—or "Beaver" as he was called, sometimes not too affectionately—to the newly created position of Minister of Aircraft Production.

The Beaver, a bustling, ruthless man of action, rolled up his sleeves and plunged into the morass of bureaucratic inefficiencies that were stifling aircraft production. Thanks to his efforts, Britain's aircraft production rose from three thousand warplanes in 1938 to fifteen thousand in 1939. Over the next two years—largely under Beaverbrook's direction—aircraft production tripled, then doubled on top of that by March 1944.

Under William Maxwell Aitken's direction, British aircraft production rose significantly during World War II.

From May to August 1940, just before and during the Battle of Britain, aircraft manufacturers under contract to the Beaver's Ministry of Aircraft Production turned out an amazing 1,875 fighter planes, compared to only 638 fighters in the previous eight months. "I saw my reserves slipping away like sand in an hour glass," Air Chief Marshal Sir Hugh C. T. Dowding, commander in chief of Britain's Fighter Command, noted later. "Without [Beaverbrook's] drive behind me I could not have carried on the battle."[71]

Dowding's Fighter Command turned away the Luftwaffe in the Battle of Britain, and a share of the RAF victory belonged to the Beaver. His war effort—a miracle of sorts—had kept them flying.

A Soviet Miracle

Another miracle of production, this one in the Soviet Union, occurred between July and December 1941. The Soviets moved 1,523 industrial firms endangered by the advancing German armies—mostly steel, iron, and engineering plants—eastward to the Urals, to the Volga region, to Kazakhstan in central Asia, and to eastern Siberia. Soviet railways bore 1.5 million wagon loads of machines and equipment to the east, along with an estimated 16.5 million Soviet citizens—plant workers, managers, and engineers—to reassemble the plants and keep them running. This massive relocation spared the Soviet war production effort from certain disaster in 1942.

Richard Overy, professor of modern history at King's College, London, and historian of World War II, notes:

By 1942 the eastern zones supplied three-quarters of all Soviet weapons and almost all the iron and steel. The restoration of economic order out of chaos and confusion caused by the German assault was as remarkable as the revival of Red Army fortunes after Stalingrad, and just as essential to the Allied cause.[72]

Simplicity of Soviet weaponry helped Soviet industry to meet and exceed goals set by the State Defense Committee. The Soviets concentrated on producing two main types of tanks, the T-34 and the KV, and five types of aircraft, one bomber, one fighter-bomber, and three fighters. In 1942 Soviet planners ordered the production of twenty-two thousand tanks and the same number of aircraft; Soviet workers in the eastern sites produced twenty-five thousand of each.

In a way, it is possible to argue that Soviet workers were the real heroes of their nation's fight against the Nazis. As the war wore on, the output of each worker in Soviet war industry increased two- to threefold. This, despite the fact that workers subsisted on only a pound of bread and a few scraps of meat and fat a day. The most and best of everything went to soldiers fighting at the front.

From a low point in 1941, Soviet tank strength climbed steadily, to double that of the Germans by the end of 1942, and triple German tank numbers by the fall of 1943. Soviet airpower enjoyed a similar climb. After losing most of its aircraft to the Luftwaffe in 1941, the Soviet air arm finished the war with some eleven thousand frontline aircraft.

Although Stalin exhorted the people to greater and greater effort in the so-called Great Patriotic War, his urgings were not really needed. As one Soviet citizen later commented:

> The best time of our lives was the War because we all felt closer to our government than at any other time in our lives. It was not *they* who wanted this or that to be done, but *we* who wanted to do it. It was not *their* war, but *our* war. It was *our* country we were defending, *our* war effort.[73]

And it was the people who—through Soviet central planning, mass mobilization, and mass production—salvaged a near-collapsed war economy and turned it into the world's second greatest producer of war goods. *Theirs* was also some kind of miracle.

American Industry Goes to War

Perhaps the American people and the United States fostered the greatest war-production miracle of all time. From the onset of the war, Britain had held on grimly, hoping that American intervention would inevitably bring enormous resources and productivity to bear against the Axis forces. In October 1941 British economist Sir William Layton, commenting on Germany's dominance over Britain in steel production, told an audience of American industrialists, "There is one way, and one way only, in which the three to one ratio of Germany's steel output can be overwhelmed and that is by the 50 to 60 million ingot tons of the United States."[74] Moreover, the United States then produced more steel, aluminum, oil, and motor vehicles than all the other major nations combined.

These figures sound impressive but are deceptive in that, after two decades of disarmament and isolationism, the world's richest nation could field an army ranked only eighteenth in the world and was able to muster an air force of barely twenty thousand men and seventeen hundred largely vintage aircraft. Moreover, only 2 percent of the U.S. gross national product had been allocated to the military in 1940.

In a message to Congress on June 10, 1941, President Franklin D. Roosevelt vowed, "With our national resources, our productive capacity, and the genius of our people for mass-production we will . . . outstrip the Axis powers in munitions of war."[75] American production expertise had hitherto been concentrated almost entirely in the commercial sector and was not refocused on an earnest rearmament effort until 1942. But once American industry was rechanneled into a war-production mode, the balance of power between America and its Axis enemies shifted virtually overnight.

American automobile companies manufactured nearly all of the tanks used during the war. Here, tanks are mass-produced at a Detroit Chrysler plant.

In 1942, essentially America's first year in the arms business, the United States outproduced the combined Axis nations, 47,000 aircraft to 27,000, 24,000 tanks to 11,000, and heavy guns by a ratio of 6 to 1. The General Motors Corporation alone met one-tenth of the nation's arms quotas. By 1945 the automobile industry together supplied one-fifth of American military equipment—almost all tanks and vehicles, one-third of the machine guns, and nearly two-fifths of aviation supplies. In four years U.S. shipyards produced 8,800 warships and 87,000 landing craft. America had truly become what President Roosevelt had once requested of it: "the great arsenal of democracy." [76]

America's conversion from producing refrigerators and washing machines to tanks and aircraft carriers owed much of its success to the expertise, imagination, and leadership of private-sector entrepreneurs, and to the diligence and dedication of the American workforce.

The Speer Miracle

As for Germany's war production, Hitler began the war three to four years too early. The rebuilding of the nation's economy and armed forces following World War I was still in a state of lengthy and costly construction when the führer opted to launch World War II in Poland. Had he waited until the mid-1940s to unleash his war machine, Germany might have by then become the world's first superpower, un-

Millions of American women responded to Roosevelt's call for wartime munitions by joining the workforce.

stoppable even by the collective might of the Allies. But Hitler was impatient to deliver living space to the German people and to lay his hands on the bountiful resources in the eastern territories.

Hitler also overestimated his personal importance and feared that he might not live long enough to see his dream—the Nazi dream—come true. He argued that the war must not be delayed because "essentially all depends on me, on my existence, because of my political talents. . . . But I can be eliminated at any time by a criminal or lunatic. No one knows how much longer I shall live. Therefore, better a conflict now."[77]

Germany had sufficient reserves of arms and resources built up to sustain itself for the first two years of the war, and it still received a flow of resources from the parts of the Soviet Union it had occupied. The war went well for the Germans as long as their blitzkrieg campaigns were crushing near-defenseless nations in their path. But modern wars are also fought and won in the factories, laboratories, schools, and supply centers on the home front. Hitler appeared to understand this when he wrote, "Modern warfare is above all economic warfare, and the demands of economic warfare must be given priority."[78] Yet, as the man in charge, he failed to fully mobilize the German economy to counter the probability of a prolonged war of attrition (a gradual reduction of forces and resources).

On paper, the German military-industrial production system appeared to be a model of efficiency. In reality, it was a morass of competing personalities and bureaucracies. Only Hitler's appointment of Albert Speer as Minister of Armaments and War Production in 1942 forestalled the collapse of Germany's wartime economy.

Speer, with Hitler's backing, assumed complete control over the entire war economy. He established a central planning board and a system of "organized improvisation" to mobilize the economy for total war. Speer later explained:

> We formed "directive committees" for the various types of weapons and "directive pools" for the allocation of supplies. Thirteen such committees were finally established, one for each category of my armaments program. Linking these were an equal number of pools. . . . The heads of the committees and pools were to make sure—this was vital to our whole approach—that a given plant concentrated on producing only one item, but did so in maximum quantity.[79]

War production soared, even in the face of Allied bombing, reaching a peak in September 1944. But then the Allied bombing campaign directed at Germany proper began in earnest.

Under a steady onslaught of Allied bombs, conditions on the German home front deteriorated rapidly. Forced laborers made up more and more of the workforce—7 million, or one-quarter of the workforce by late 1944. Since the SS supplied the forced labor, Himmler's influence over the war economy rose steadily, undermining Speer's authority and all but guaranteeing the collapse of his revitalized German war economy. The "Speer miracle," as the resurgence of German war production was known—and that was achievable only through the ruthless exploitation of human and material resources from occupied Europe—ended in the early months of 1945. Only a major miracle could now salvage the Nazi dream and save Germany from certain defeat.

An Absurd Notion

The development and utilization of German high-technology weaponry failed in many instances because of interference from Hitler. In *Inside the Third Reich*, German armaments and production minister Albert Speer cites two examples:

> We were literally suffering from an excess of projects in development. Had we concentrated on only a few types we would surely have completed some of them sooner. . . .

> Once again it was Hitler who, in spite of all the tactical mistakes of the Allies, ordained those very moves which helped the enemy air offensive in 1944 achieve its successes. After postponing the development of the jet fighter [Me-262] and later converting it into a light bomber, Hitler now decided to use our big new rockets to retaliate against England. From the end of July 1943 on tremendous industrial capacity was diverted to the huge missile later known as the V-2; a rocket forty-six feet long and weighing more than thirteen metric tons. Hitler wanted to have nine hundred of these produced monthly.

> The whole notion was absurd. The fleets of enemy bombers in 1944 were dropping an average of three thousand tons of bombs a day over a span of several months. And Hitler wanted to retaliate with thirty rockets that would have carried twenty-four tons of explosives daily. That was equivalent to the bomb load of only twelve Flying Fortresses.

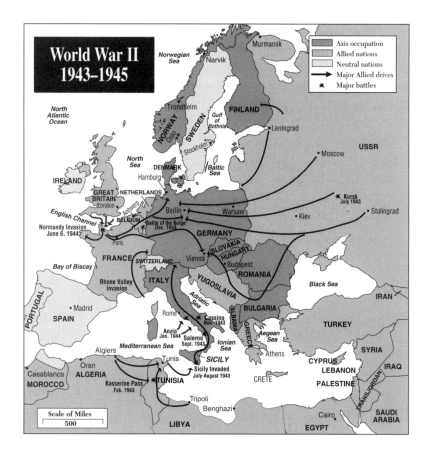

Secret Weapons

As the war started turning against Germany, Hitler clung to his belief that German science would devise a new generation of weaponry that in a single stroke would bring about a reversal of Germany's military fortunes. As early as February 1944, Joseph Goebbels sought to re-assure Nazi Party leaders that Germany would soon snatch victory from defeat using a secret weapon. "Retribution is at hand. It will take a form hitherto unknown in warfare, a form the enemy will find impossible to bear." [80] Goebbels was alluding to an atomic bomb, the development of which eluded the best scientific minds in Germany.

Later in the year, Himmler urged the renewal of atomic bomb re-search and the development of "N-material," a new chemical weapon that was literally inextinguishable. Hitler himself, at a time when men and materials might have been put to better use in more conventional pursuits, encouraged crash scientific projects. With defeat staring him in the face, however, such efforts proved too little and too late.

German scientists under Wernher von Braun (who would live to become a key figure in U.S. postwar space endeavors) developed the V-1 flying bomb and the V-2 rocket, the world's first intercontinental ballistic missile. (The "V" stood for "vengeance.") Hitler, enraged by Allied bombings of Munich, pledged vengeance to his mistress Eva Braun:

> Panic will break out in England! The effect of this weapon [the V-2] will be too much for anyone's nerves. I shall pay back those barbarians who are now massacring women and children and destroying German culture.[81]

The "vengeance" weapons achieved tactical success by terrorizing a few communities in Britain and Belgium during 1944 and 1945, but failed strategically in that they did not stave off Germany's defeat. These weapons were simply too inaccurate to be effective. Of some eight thousand V-2s fired at England, fewer than one-fifth struck their target.

Other promising weapons fell victim to Hitler's meddling. The Messerschmitt Me-262, the world's first turbojet fighter, was potentially the most viable of Germany's secret weapons. But as was the

The German V-1 "vengeance" flying bomb, shown here in 1946, proved to be too inaccurate to be effective.

The Messerschmitt Me-262—the first jet flown in combat—had little impact on the outcome of the war.

case in so many areas and in so many instances, Hitler intervened both in its development and application. Albert Speer recalled:

> Hitler indicated that he planned to use the plane, which was built to be a fighter, as a fast bomber. The air force specialists were dismayed. . . .

> The fact that these planes could fly higher than American escort fighters and could attack the relatively clumsy American bomber squadrons at will because of their immensely superior speed made no impression at all on Hitler.[82]

Hitler's interference delayed production of the Me-262 until early 1944. The first jet-fighter unit was not formed until the following November. By then, fuel shortages disrupted pilot training. In the end, fewer than 250 Me-262s were flown in combat. Had the jets been available in June 1944, the Germans might well have thrown the Allies off the beaches of Normandy.

The *Grofaz* had erred again. Amid the thunder of Allied bombings—which the Me-262s might have stopped had it not been for Hitler—Germany's cities were being pummeled into rubble. And the Nazi dream had become a nightmare.

The Final Reckoning

Epilogue

The moral forces are amongst the most important subjects in War. They form the spirit which permeates the whole being of War. These forces fasten themselves soonest and with the greatest affinity onto the Will which puts in motion and guides the whole mass of powers, uniting with it as it were one stream, because this [the Will] is a moral force itself.

—Carl von Clausewitz, *On War*

IN THE END, A major factor in the success of the Allies lay in their ability to identify clear objectives that were meaningful to the vast majority of their citizens. By so doing, the Allies provided their people with national incentives predicated on such themes as "right over might" and "freedom for all." Such incentives fostered an enduring inner strength—a will to win—in the minds and hearts of the Allied rank and file. The renowned military strategist Carl von Clausewitz called this vital moral force "national feeling."[83]

Winston Churchill recognized the importance of national feeling, that is, patriotic spirit, and repeatedly delivered rousing speeches designed to bolster that spirit in Britons and harness the national will against the forces of Axis evil. During the evacuation of British and French forces at Dunkirk, three weeks before the fall of France, he addressed the House of Commons and vowed: "We shall go on to the end . . . we shall fight on the beaches, we shall fight on the landing-grounds, we shall fight in the fields and in the streets . . . we shall never surrender."[84] The plucky prime minister's stirring oratory galvanized the will of the British people and sustained them through their darkest hours and throughout the war.

Soviet dictator Joseph Stalin also recognized the value of patriotic spirit and repeatedly implored his people to fight for Mother Russia in the centuries-old war of Slavs against Germans. Soviet soldiers were often known to charge into battle shouting, "For Motherland and Stalin!"[85]

President Roosevelt, a gifted orator and motivational leader, established America's future war aims in his annual address to Congress on January 6, 1941—almost a year before the United States entered the war. In a ringing conclusion to his speech, he declared that democracies were responsible for defending the "four essential human freedoms,"[86] which he expressed as freedom of speech and religion, and freedom from want and fear.

These four freedoms—later lionized in four paintings by American folk artist Norman Rockwell—represented basic values worth fighting for then and since and cleared the way for America's involvement in World War II. Eleven months later Americans carried these values into the battle, firm in the knowledge that these freedoms were worth defending.

Winston Churchill's moving speeches inspired patriotism in the British people and galvanized support for the war effort.

Americans rallied behind President Roosevelt and his fight to preserve human freedoms.

Germany's Moral Decline

In contrast to motivations of the Allies that stemmed from the need to defend their nations against Axis aggressions, the Germans went to war under banners of conquest and world domination. Although many Germans opposed the war, albeit passively, or entered into it with misgivings, early Axis victories provided a moral lift to most Germans. But as the war wore on with little indication from Axis authorities as to the nature of war aims or the moral justification for them, Axis populations underwent a growing demoralization.

In Germany support for the war started declining as early as October 1941, when Hitler failed to deliver on his promise to defeat the Soviet Union. This necessitated increasingly brutal regimentation on the home front. The Italians surrendered readily in 1943, and amid the chaos and rubble of Allied bombings, the quest for *Lebensraum* and the promise of a New Order in Europe lost its appeal in Germany. In Berlin desperation set in.

When the war on the Eastern Front turned against them, the Nazis tried frantically to sustain public moral support with a new approach: they would seek moral justification on the home front by discarding the premise of an aggressive war for living space. Instead, they would rally the people under the standard of a life-or-death clash between European civilization, safeguarded by Germany, and the savage Slavic hordes of the east. This was a compelling argument for the Germans to fight harder, and for a time they did.

Speaking for Hitler at Berlin's Sports Palace, Joseph Goebbels warned, "In this war there will be neither victors nor vanquished, but only survivors and annihilated."[87] It became clear to the German people that victory was no longer at issue; what mattered now was survival. This was a moral incentive for them to fight on, but one that held little of the animating qualities of the enemy's more idealistic motivations. Also, for the tens of thousands of Germans who participated in the slaughter of millions of Jews, Slavs, Gypsies, and others, plus related barbarisms, surrender was no option. In this atmosphere of moral decline, the outcome of the war became totally predictable.

Hastening Hitler's Doom

The Allies hastened the end of the war with an accelerated bombing campaign, which brought the Allies' own moral values into serious

Moral Forces

Soldier and military theorist Carl von Clausewitz expounds on the nature of war activities in his famous treatise *On War*. He lends particular emphasis to "moral forces and their effects (hostile feeling)," shown here in part:

> The combat is, in its origin, the expression of *hostile feeling,* but in our great combats, which we call Wars, the hostile feeling frequently resolves itself into merely a hostile *view,* and there is no innate hostile feeling residing in individual against individual. Nevertheless, the combat never passes off without such feelings being brought into activity. National hatred, which is seldom wanting in our Wars, is a substitute for personal hostility in the breast of individual opposed to individual. But where this also is wanting, and at first no animosity exists, a hostile feeling is kindled by the combat itself; for an act of violence which anyone commits upon us by order of his superior, will excite in us a desire to retaliate and be revenged on him, sooner than on the superior power at whose command the act was done. This is human, or animal if we will; still it is so.

question. In the summer of 1944, the British proposed a joint Anglo-American bombing raid of overwhelming strength on Berlin, so massive that it would yield a toll of some 275,000 killed or injured. Code-named Thunderclap, the operation was aimed at shattering German civilian morale.

Although the Americans had generally tried to distance themselves from the Royal Air Force's "area" attacks—RAF jargon for terror bombings—the concept had long intrigued American air planners. But American air force commander Carl A. Spaatz was not a proponent of the concept. He advised General Dwight D. Eisenhower, supreme commander of Allied forces in Europe, that Thunderclap was an attempt by the RAF "to have the U.S. tarred with the morale bombing aftermath which we feel will be terrific."[88] Spaatz did not want his air force to be tarred with the brush of immoral bombings of helpless civilians.

Eisenhower admitted that he favored precision bombing, presumedly of military targets, then, alarmingly replied, "I am always

The Central Moral Problem

In 1947 former U.S. secretary of war Henry L. Stimson wrote of his concerns about the increasing brutality of war. The following paragraph appears in Albert Speer's *Inside the Third Reich:*

> We must never forget, that under modern conditions of life, science, and technology, all war has become increasingly brutalized, and that no one who joins in it, even in self-defense, can escape becoming also in a measure brutalized. Modern war cannot be limited in its destructive method and the inevitable debasement of all participants. . . . A fair scrutiny of the last two World Wars makes clear the steady intensification in the inhumanity of the weapons and methods employed by both, the aggressors and the victors. In order to defeat Japanese aggression, we were forced, as Admiral Nimitz [commander in chief, Pacific] has stated, to employ a technique of unrestricted submarine warfare, not unlike that which 25 years ago was the proximate cause of our entry into World War I. In the use of strategic air power the Allies took the lives of hundreds of thousands of civilians in Germany and Japan. . . . We as well as our enemies have contributed to the proof that the central moral problem is war and not its methods, and that a continuance of war will in all probability end with the destruction of our civilization.

General Dwight D. Eisenhower gives orders to paratrooopers in England as they prepare to invade Europe in June 1944.

prepared to take part in anything that gives real promise to ending the war quickly." [89] As a result of Eisenhower's decision, an Anglo-American raid on February 3, 1945, killed twenty-five thousand civilians. A similar bombing raid on Dresden ten days later touched off a firestorm that claimed the lives of thirty-five thousand people by both flames and suffocation. The moral firestorm resulting from such bombings still rages.

In an effort to downplay American participation in the attacks, U.S. authorities asserted that both raids had been directed against military targets only. The *St. Louis Post-Dispatch* did not accept official disclaimers, describing the Allied decision to bomb population centers this way: "Allied air bosses have made the long-awaited decision to adopt deliberate terror bombing of the great German population centers as a ruthless expedient to hasten Hitler's doom." [90] Following behind advancing Allied armies in western Europe, the

The Anglo-American bombing raid on Dresden razed the city and left thirty-five thousand people dead.

United States Strategic Bombing Survey conducted 208 separate studies into the air strategists' claims that airpower was decisive in Germany's defeat. The survey concluded that bombing had contributed significantly to the Allied victory but had not by itself proved decisive. But the bombings did demonstrate that the Allies did not always opt to soar on the highest moral plane.

A Fateful Irony

In the final reckoning, Hitler thought that strength of will or willpower could prevail over vast supplies of weapons and war matériels. Ironically, his conviction held true not for him and his Nazi brethren but rather for their adversaries. As the eminent British historian Richard Overy so astutely points out:

The irony was that Hitler's ambition to impose his will on others did perhaps more than anything to ensure that his enemies' will to win burned brighter still. The Allies were united by nothing so much as a fundamental desire to smash Hitlerism . . . and to use any weapon to achieve it. This primal drive for victory at all costs nourished Allied fighting power and assuaged the thirst for vengeance. They fought not only because the sum of their resources added up to victory, but because they wanted to win and were certain that their cause was just.[91]

Hitler tried to impose a new morality on the world—one rooted in hatred, racism, barbarism, terrorism, and enslavement—and he failed. And so failed the Nazi dream.

● ● ● ●

On April 30, 1945, Adolf Hitler shot and killed himself in the Führer Bunker beneath the German chancellery in Berlin. Unlike other movements of world import that have survived their creator, Nazism died an instant death.

Notes

Introduction: The Nazis and Their Dream

1. Quoted in John Toland, *Adolf Hitler*. New York: Anchor Books, 1992, p. 291.
2. Quoted in Toland, *Adolf Hitler*, p. 291.
3. Quoted in William L. Shirer, *The Rise and Fall of the Third Reich*. New York: Simon & Schuster, 1960, p. 5.
4. Quoted in Shirer, *The Rise and Fall of the Third Reich*, p. 5.
5. Adolf Hitler, *Mein Kampf*. Translated by Ralph Mannheim. Boston: Houghton Mifflin, 1971, p. 327.
6. Quoted in Louis L. Snyder, *Encyclopedia of the Third Reich*. New York: Paragon House, 1989, p. 106.
7. Hitler, *Mein Kampf*, p. 383.
8. Hitler, *Mein Kampf*, p. 57.
9. Hitler, *Mein Kampf*, p. 654.

Chapter 1: Hitler's Leadership: Mistakes on a Grand Scale

10. Quoted in Snyder, *Encyclopedia of the Third Reich*, p. 171.
11. Quoted in Gerhard L. Weinberg, *Germany, Hitler, and World War II: Essays in Modern German and World History*. New York: Cambridge University Press, 1995, p. 155.
12. Quoted in Shirer, *The Rise and Fall of the Third Reich*, p. 318.
13. Quoted in Toland, *Adolf Hitler*, p. 431.
14. Quoted in Time-Life Books editors, *WW II: Time-Life History of the Second World War*. New York: Barnes & Noble, 1995, p. 52.
15. Quoted in Norman Polmar and Thomas B. Allen, *World War II: The Encyclopedia of the War Years 1941–1945*. New York: Random House, 1996, p. 614.
16. Quoted in Matthew Cooper, *The German Army, 1933–1945: Its*

Political and Military Failure. Military Book Club edition. USA: Scarborough House, (undated), p. 107.

17. Quoted in Edward Jablonski, *A Pictorial History of the World War II Years*. New York: Wings Books, 1995, p. 21.
18. Quoted in Snyder, *Encyclopedia of the Third Reich*, p. 164.
19. Quoted in Sidney C. Moody Jr. and the Associated Press, *War in Europe*. Novato, CA: Presidio Press, 1993, p. 27.
20. Quoted in Albert Speer, *Inside the Third Reich*. New York: Galahad Books, 1995, p. 170.
21. Winston Churchill, *Their Finest Hour*, vol. 2, The Second World War. Boston: Houghton Mifflin, 1948, p. 217.
22. Quoted in Jablonski, *A Pictorial History of the World War II Years*, p. 83.
23. Quoted in Toland, *Adolf Hitler*, p. 690.
24. Quoted in Klaus P. Fischer, *Nazi Germany: A New History*. New York: Continuum, 1995, p. 474.
25. Quoted in Toland, *Adolf Hitler*, p. 695.
26. Quoted in Fischer, *Nazi Germany*, p. 478.
27. Quoted in Time-Life Books editors, *WW II*, p. 207.
28. Speer, *Inside the Third Reich*, p. 473.
29. Quoted in Fischer, *Nazi Germany*, p. 563.

Chapter 2: *Der Führer* and *Il Duce:* A Flawed Friendship

30. Hitler, *Mein Kampf*, p. 3.
31. Quoted in Toland, *Adolf Hitler*, pp. 354–55.
32. William L. Shirer, *Berlin Diary: The Journal of a Foreign Correspondent, 1934–1941*. New York: Galahad Books, 1995, p. 43.
33. Quoted in Shirer, *The Rise and Fall of the Third Reich*, p. 298.
34. Quoted in Fischer, *Nazi Germany*, p. 421.
35. Quoted in John Weitz, *Hitler's Diplomat: The Life and Times of Joachim von Ribbentrop*. New York: Ticknor & Fields, 1992, p. 214.
36. Quoted in Shirer, *The Rise and Fall of the Third Reich*, p. 556.
37. Quoted in Weitz, *Hitler's Diplomat*, pp. 234–35.
38. Quoted in Time-Life Books editors, *WW II*, p. 214.
39. Quoted in Weitz, *Hitler's Diplomat*, p. 256.

Chapter 3: Barbarossa: War on Two Fronts

40. Quoted in Philip Kaplin and Richard Collier, *Their Finest Hour:*

The Battle of Britain Remembered. New York: Abbeville Press, 1989, p. 191.

41. Hitler, *Mein Kampf*, pp. 654–55.
42. Quoted in Jon E. Lewis, ed., *The Mammoth Book of Battles*. New York: Carroll & Graf, 1995, p. 184.
43. Quoted in Moody and the Associated Press, *War in Europe*, p. 58.
44. Quoted in Churchill, *Their Finest Hour*, pp. 589–90.
45. Quoted in Jablonski, *A Pictorial History of the World War II Years*, p. 84.
46. Quoted in Toland, *Adolf Hitler*, p. 651.
47. Quoted in Time-Life Books editors, *WW II*, p. 120.
48. Quoted in Toland, *Adolf Hitler*, p. 675.
49. Quoted in Jablonski, *A Pictorial History of the World War II Years*, p. 87.
50. Quoted in Time-Life Books editors, *WW II*, p. 130.
51. Quoted in Moody and the Associated Press, *War in Europe*, p. 59.
52. Quoted in Moody and the Associated Press, *War in Europe*, p. 59.
53. Quoted in Fischer, *Nazi Germany*, p. 472.
54. Quoted in Time-Life Books editors, *WW II*, p. 132.
55. Quoted in Fischer, *Nazi Germany*, p. 473.
56. Quoted in Moody and the Associated Press, *War in Europe*, p. 56.

Chapter 4: The Holocaust: A Despicable Diversion

57. Quoted in Leni Yahil, *The Holocaust: The Fate of European Jewry*. Translated by Ina Friedman and Haya Galai. New York: Oxford University Press, 1990, pp. 254–55.
58. Quoted in Lucy S. Dawidowicz, *The War Against the Jews, 1933--1945*. New York: Bantam Books, 1986, p. 69.
59. Hitler, *Mein Kampf*, p. 402.
60. Quoted in Rupert Butler, *An Illustrated History of the Gestapo*. London: Wordwright Books, 1996, p. 38.
61. Quoted in Dawidowicz, *The War Against the Jews*, p. 120.
62. Quoted in Snyder, *Encyclopedia of the Third Reich*, p. 145.
63. Quoted in Time-Life Books editors, *The SS*, vol. 2, The Third Reich series. Alexandria, VA: Time-Life Books, 1989, p. 122.
64. Quoted in Martin Gilbert, *The Holocaust: A History of the Jews of Europe During the Second World War*. New York: Henry Holt, 1987, p. 203.

65. Quoted in Yahil, *The Holocaust*, p. 257.

66. Quoted in Robert Jay Lifton, *The Nazi Doctors: Medical Killing and the Psychology of Genocide*. New York: BasicBooks, 1986, p. 159.

67. Rudolf Höss, *Death Dealer: The Memoirs of the SS Kommandant at Auschwitz*. Translated by A. Pollinger. New York: Da Capo Press, 1996, p. 242.

68. Quoted in Dawidowicz, *The War Against the Jews,* p. 144.

Chapter 5: The Clash of Economies and Technology

69. Quoted in Moody and the Associated Press, *War in Europe*, p. 191.

70. Quoted in Kaplin and Collier, *Their Finest Hour*, p. 25.

71. Quoted in Kaplin and Collier, *Their Finest Hour*, p. 26.

72. Richard Overy, *Why the Allies Won*. New York: W. W. Norton, 1995, p. 181.

73. Quoted in Time-Life Books editors, *WW II*, p. 191.

74. Quoted in Overy, *Why the Allies Won*, p. 190.

75. Quoted in Overy, *Why the Allies Won*, p. 180.

76. Quoted in Stephen E. Ambrose and C. L. Sulzberger, *American Heritage New History of World War II*. New York: Viking, 1997, p. 115.

77. Quoted in Fischer, *Nazi Germany*, p. 441.

78. Quoted in Fischer, *Nazi Germany*, p. 442.

79. Speer, *Inside the Third Reich*, p. 208.

80. Quoted in Overy, *Why the Allies Won*, p. 243.

81. Quoted in Toland, *Adolf Hitler*, p. 781.

82. Speer, *Inside the Third Reich*, p. 363.

Epilogue: The Final Reckoning

83. Carl von Clausewitz, *On War*. Edited with an introduction by Anatol Rapoport. New York: Penguin Books, 1968, p. 253.

84. Churchill, *Their Finest Hour*, p. 118.

85. Quoted in Overy, *Why the Allies Won*, p. 292.

86. Quoted in David M. Kennedy, *Freedom from Fear: The American People in Depression and War, 1929–1945*. The Oxford History of the United States. New York: Oxford University Press, 1999, p. 469.

87. Quoted in Overy, *Why the Allies Won*, p. 306.
88. Quoted in Kennedy, *Freedom from Fear*, p. 744.
89. Quoted in Kennedy, *Freedom from Fear*, p. 744.
90. Quoted in Kennedy, *Freedom from Fear*, p. 744.
91. Quoted in Overy, *Why the Allies Won*, p. 325.

Chronology

1889
April 20: Birth of Adolf Hitler in Braunau-am-Inn, Austria.

1919
June 28: Treaty of Versailles signed, officially ending World War I.

1922
October 22: Mussolini seizes power in Rome.

1933
January 30: Hitler appointed chancellor of Germany; birth of the Third Reich.

1934
March 17: Mussolini concludes pact of cooperation with Austria and Hungary.

July 25: Austrian chancellor Engelbert Dollfuss assassinated.

August 12: President Paul von Hindenburg dies; Hitler declares himself both the chancellor and *Der Führer* of the Third Reich and becomes the absolute dictator of Germany.

1935
March 16: Hitler abrogates the Treaty of Versailles.

October 3: Italy invades Abyssinia (Ethiopia).

1936
March 7: Hitler reclaims the demilitarized Rhineland for Germany.

May 2: Italian troops enter the Abyssinian capital of Addis Ababa.

July 16: General Francisco Franco stages an armed revolt in Spain; Spanish civil war begins.

October 21: Rome-Berlin Axis agreement signed in Berlin.

1937

November 5: Hossbach Conference; Hitler outlines plans for achieving living space (*Lebensraum*) by force.

1938

February 4: Hitler creates the *Oberkommando der Wehrmacht*, or OKW—the high command of the armed forces—and appoints himself as its supreme commander.

March 12–13: Germany annexes Austria (the *Anschluss*).

September 29–30: Munich Conference; Britain and France cede Sudetenland (in Czechoslovakia) to Germany.

1939

March 13–14: Germany occupies the rest of Czechoslovakia and establishes protectorates in Bohemia, Moravia, and Slovakia.

March 31: Britain and France pledge to guarantee Poland's security and territorial integrity.

April 3: Hitler issues directive for *Fall Weiss* (Case White), calling for the invasion of Poland and the destruction of the Polish armed forces.

May 22: Germany and Italy sign the Pact of Steel.

May 23: Hitler informs senior officers that war is unavoidable.

August 23: Hitler-Stalin Pact signed, a nonaggression agreement between Germany and the Soviet Union.

August 25: Mussolini reneges on Pact of Steel.

September 1: Germany invades Poland; World War II begins.

September 3: Britain and France declare war on Germany.

1940

March 10: Hitler urges Mussolini to enter the war.

June 10: Italy declares war on Britain and France.

June 22: Franco-German armistice.

July 10–October 31: Battle of Britain.

September 13: Italians launch an offensive in North Africa aimed at Cairo.

September 17: Hitler postpones Operation Sea Lion (the invasion of Britain).

September 27: Germany, Italy, and Japan sign Tripartite Pact, promising mutual military aid.

October 28: Italy invades Greece.

1941

May 15: Original planned start date for Operation Barbarossa (the invasion of the Soviet Union).

June 10: Roosevelt vows to "outstrip the Axis powers in munitions of war."

June 22: Hitler launches Operation Barbarossa.

July 31: Göring issues "final solution" directive to Heydrich.

August 5: Smolensk falls to Germans.

September 16: Kiev capitulates to Germans; Hitler retargets Moscow as the primary German objective.

October 2: Germans launch Operation Typhoon (the final drive on Moscow).

December 2: German offensive stalls within sight of the Kremlin.

December 6: Soviets launch counterattack outside Moscow.

December 7: Japan attacks Pearl Harbor.

December 11: Hitler declares war on the United States.

1942

January 20: The Wannsee Conference convenes to plan the "final solution" to the Jewish question.

November 11: British break through at El Alamein, Egypt; Field Marshal Erwin Rommel's Afrika Korps retreats across Libya.

1943

January 31: German Sixth Army surrenders at Stalingrad.

July 25: Mussolini deposed in Rome.

1944

June 6: Allies land in Normandy (Operation Overlord).

December 16–January 28, 1945: Battle of the Bulge.

1945

February 3: Allies bomb civilian population of Berlin.

February 13: Allies bomb civilian population of Dresden.

April 30: Hitler commits suicide in his Berlin bunker.

May 7: Germany formally surrenders; the Third Reich ends.

May 8: V-E Day (Victory in Europe Day).

Glossary

Afrika Korps: German forces in North Africa.

Anschluss: Union; German annexation of Austria.

Aryan: Hypothetical ethnic type used by the Nazis to designate a supposed master race of non-Jewish Caucasians having especially Nordic features.

Axis: Political and military alliance of chiefly Germany, Italy, and Japan in World War II.

Beer Hall Putsch: Abortive attempt by Hitler and his new Nazi Party to overthrow the Bavarian government by force in 1923; put down by Bavarian armed forces and state police.

blitzkrieg: Lightning war.

chancellor: Chief minister of state in some European countries.

China Incident: Japanese euphemism for the Sino-Japanese War (1937–1945).

Die Endlösung: The Final Solution.

Directive 21: Hitler's war directive initiating **Operation Barbarossa**.

Duce, Il: The Leader (Italian); Italian dictator Benito Mussolini's self-styled title.

Einsatzgruppen: Task forces; German mobile killing units.

Einsatzkommandos: Killing units; subdivisions of *Einsatzgruppen.*

Fall Fritz: Case Fritz; original name for **Operation Barbarossa.**

Fall Weiss: Case White; Hitler's plan for the invasion of Poland.

fascism: A centralized, oppressive government, headed by a dictator, that exalts nation and often race above the individual.

Final Solution: Nazi euphemism for the annihilation of the Jews of Europe; *Die Endlösung; see also* **Holocaust.**

Führer, Der: The Leader (German); Hitler's self-proclaimed title as supreme ruler of Germany's Third Reich.

Führerprinzip: Leadership principle; Hitler's concept that Germany must be an authoritarian state with power emanating from a leader at the top.

Gesammtlösung: The overall solution to the Jewish question.

Gesetz sum Schutze des deutschen Blutes und des deutschen Ehre: Law for the Protection of German Blood and Honor.

Gleichschaltung: Cooperation; Nazi concept dedicated to unifying all aspects of German life and culture in a racially pure Aryan community.

Grofaz: Grosster Fedheer Allen Zeiten, or greatest military commander of all time; title sometimes assigned to Hitler, sometimes derisively.

Hitler-Stalin Pact: Nonaggression agreement between Germany and the Soviet Union signed on August 23, 1939.

Holocaust: Name for the physical destruction of 6 million Jews during World War II; *see also* **Final Solution.**

"Horst Wessel Lied": "Horst Wessel Song"; the official marching song of the Nazi Party, named for its lyricist.

Hossbach Conference: Meeting held at the Reich Chancellery on November 5, 1937, during which Hitler outlined his plans for obtaining living space (*Lebensraum*) by force.

Kanzler: **chancellor.**

League of Nations: An international organization formed after World War I to promote world peace and security.

Lebensraum: Living space; Hitler's doctrine of expanding Germany's borders to fit its population by conquest.

Luftwaffe: German air force.

Mein Kampf: Hitler's autobiographical work; a rambling, semiliterate diatribe filled with anti-Semitism, power worship, gross immoralities, and a detailed plan for world domination; the bible of the Nazi Party.

Mischling: A part Jew.

Munich Conference: Meeting held in Munich, September 29–30, 1938, during which Britain and France appeased Hitler's expansionism by ceding the German-speaking Sudetenland of Czechoslovakia to Germany.

Nazi: From *NAtionalsoZIalist,* shortened form of *Nationalsozialistische Deutsche Arbeiterpartei* (National Socialist German Workers' Party; often abbreviated as NSDAP).

Neuordnung: **New Order.**

New Order: Hitler's concept of a total rearrangement of German life to coincide with his **Weltanschauung,** or world order (*Neuordnung*).

NSDAP: *See* **Nazi.**

Oberkommando der Wehrmacht: OKW; the high command of the German armed forces.

Operation Barbarossa: Code name for the German invasion of the Soviet Union; Hitler borrowed the name from the German hero and Holy Roman Emperor Frederick I (1123–1190), known as Barbarossa, from the Italian for "red beard"; s*ee also* **Fall Fritz.**

Operation Typhoon: The final German drive on Moscow.

Pact of Steel: Political alliance between Germany and Italy, signed in Berlin on May 22, 1939; also called the Rome-Berlin Axis.

panzer: Tank.

Polish Corridor: A narrow strip of land awarded to Poland by the Treaty of Versailles (1919), giving Poland access to the Baltic Sea but separating East Prussia from Germany proper.

Reichsbürgergesetz: Reich Citizenship Law.

Reichsführer: Reich leader; Adolf Hitler.

Reichsführer-SS: Reich leader of the SS; Heinrich Himmler.

Reichspresident: Reich president.

Reichstag: German parliament.

RSHA: *Reichssicherheitshauptamt*; Reich Central Security Office; the main security office of the Nazi government.

Schutzstaffel: The SS (literally, "defense echelon"); an elite guard of political police and soldiers; *see also* **Waffen-SS.**

"Sieg Heil!": German for "Hail to Victory!"

Sonderkommandos: Special units; subdivisions of *Einsatzgruppen.*

Third Reich: Third Empire; the official Nazi designation for the regime in power from January 1933 to May 1945; Hitler regarded it as a logical extension of Otto the Great's First Reich (circa 962) and Otto von Bismarck's Second Reich (circa 1871).

"Thousand-Year Reich": The Third Reich, which Hitler boasted would last for a thousand years.

Tiergarten: A section of Berlin, Germany, on the Spree River, known for its park with flower and zoological gardens.

Treaty of Versailles: Peace agreement ending World War I, signed at Versailles, France, on June 28, 1919.

Tripartite Pact: Political alliance signed by Germany, Italy, and Japan on September 27, 1940, promising mutual military aid.

Unterseeboot: Undersea boat, or U-boat; submarine.

V-E Day: Victory in Europe Day.

Waffen-SS: Military branch of the SS; *see also* **Schutzstaffel.**

Wehrmacht: German army.

Weltanschauung: Worldview; favorite word in the Third Reich to denote the Nazis' conception of the world, or their philosophy of life.

Wolfsschanze: Wolf's Lair; Hitler's field headquarters in Rastenburg, East Prussia.

Zyklon B: Crystallized prussic acid, used in German death camps to kill Jews and others; also spelled Cyclon or Zyclon.

For Further Reading

Halina Birenbaum, *Hope Is the Last to Die: A Coming of Age Under Nazi Terror.* Translated by David Welsh. Armonk, NY: M. E. Sharpe, 1996. A reminiscence of the author's experiences growing up under the Nazis in the Warsaw ghetto.

Christopher R. Browning, *Ordinary Men: Reserve Police Battalion 101 and the Final Solution in Poland.* New York: HarperCollins, 1993. How a unit of average, middle-aged German policemen became the murderers of tens of thousands of Jews.

Alan Bullock, *Hitler: A Study in Tyranny.* New York: HarperCollins, 1991. A comprehensive biography of the German dictator by a leading contemporary historian.

Anton Gill, *An Honourable Defeat: A History of German Resistance to Hitler, 1933–1945.* New York: Henry Holt, 1994. The story of the Germans who secretly resisted the scourge of Nazism.

Daniel Jonah Goldhagen, *Hitler's Willing Executioners: Ordinary Germans and the Holocaust.* New York: Alfred A. Knopf, 1996. A controversial new look at the Holocaust.

G. S. Graber, *The History of the SS.* New York: David McKay, 1978. How the key SS men (Himmler, Heydrich, Eichmann, and others) operated within the SS—often against each other.

Lucette Matalon Lagnado and Sheila Conn Dekel, *Children of the Flames: Dr. Josef Mengele and the Untold Story of the Twins of Auschwitz.* New York: William Morrow, 1991. The life of Auschwitz's Angel of Death told in counterpoint to the surviving twins of Auschwitz; evocative and poignant.

Callum MacDonald, *The Killing of SS Obergruppenführer Reinhard Heydrich.* New York: Macmillan, 1989. An in-depth account of the only successful assassination of a leading Nazi during World War II.

Joseph E. Persico, *Nuremberg: Infamy on Trial.* New York: Penguin Books, 1995. The trial of the Nazi warlords of World War II.

Anthony Read and David Fisher, *Kristallnacht: The Unleashing of the Holocaust.* New York: Peter Bedrick Books, 1989. The story of the event that ignited the engine of the Holocaust.

Gita Sereny, *Albert Speer: His Battle with Truth.* New York: Alfred A. Knopf, 1995. A totally absorbing look at the only Nazi to take responsibility for his crimes at the Nuremberg trials.

Telford Taylor, *The Anatomy of the Nuremberg Trials.* Boston: Little, Brown, 1992. The chief prosecutor at Nuremberg recounts the trials as he heard, saw, and otherwise sensed them at the time.

Works Consulted

Stephen E. Ambrose and C. L. Sulzberger, *American Heritage New History of World War II*. New York: Viking, 1997. A masterful updating of the standard reference work.

Rupert Butler, *An Illustrated History of the Gestapo*. London: Wordwright Books, 1996. A comprehensive visual record of Hitler's dreaded henchmen.

Winston Churchill, *Their Finest Hour*. Vol. 2. The Second World War. Boston: Houghton Mifflin, 1948. Portrays England's early struggles during World War II.

————, *Triumph and Tragedy*. Vol. 6. The Second World War. Boston: Houghton Mifflin, 1953. The concluding volume to the author's panoramic history of World War II.

Carl von Clausewitz, *On War*. Edited with an introduction by Anatol Rapoport. New York: Penguin Books, 1968. The classic treatise on armed conflict.

Matthew Cooper, *The German Army, 1933–1945: Its Political and Military Failure*. Military Book Club edition. USA: Scarborough House, (undated). A sweeping, hard-hitting chronicle of the German army.

Lucy S. Dawidowicz, *The War Against the Jews, 1933–1945*. New York: Bantam Books, 1986. An unparalleled account of Hitler's attempt to eliminate European Jewry.

Klaus P. Fischer, *Nazi Germany: A New History*. New York: Continuum, 1995. Provides fresh insights into the Nazi phenomenon and the Hitlerian mystique.

Martin Gilbert, *The Holocaust: A History of the Jews of Europe During the Second World War*. New York: Henry Holt, 1987. Documents how and why the Holocaust occurred, what happened, and why it can happen again.

Whitney R. Harris, *Tyranny on Trial: The Evidence at Nuremberg*. New

York: Barnes & Noble, 1995. A detailed account of the 1945–1946 Nuremberg proceedings by one of the American prosecutors.

Adolf Hitler, *Mein Kampf*. Translated by Ralph Mannheim. Boston: Houghton Mifflin, 1971. The standard English-language translation of Hitler's autobiography.

Rudolf Höss, *Death Dealer: The Memoirs of the SS Kommandant at Auschwitz*. Translated by A. Pollinger. New York: Da Capo Press, 1996. An unexpurgated autobiography of one of history's greatest mass murderers.

Edward Jablonski, *A Pictorial History of the World War II Years*. New York: Wings Books, 1995. A highly readable, pictorial treatment of World War II.

Philip Kaplin and Richard Collier, *Their Finest Hour: The Battle of Britain Remembered*. New York: Abbeville Press, 1989. A splendidly written and illustrated look back at the pivotal battle over Britain.

David M. Kennedy, *Freedom from Fear: The American People in Depression and War, 1929–1945*. The Oxford History of the United States. New York: Oxford University Press, 1999. A comprehensive and colorful account of the most convulsive period in American history.

Jon E. Lewis, ed., *The Mammoth Book of Battles*. New York: Carroll & Graf, 1995. Battle commentaries illustrating the art and science of modern warfare.

Robert Jay Lifton, *The Nazi Doctors: Medical Killing and the Psychology of Genocide*. New York: BasicBooks, 1986. A remarkable examination into the darkest regions of the human psyche.

Sidney C. Moody Jr. and the Associated Press, *War in Europe*. Novato, CA: Presidio Press, 1993. A profusely illustrated and compelling narrative of the war.

Richard Overy, *Why the Allies Won*. New York: W. W. Norton, 1995. An examination of some of the deeper factors affecting military success and failure.

Peter Padfield, *Himmler: Reichsführer-SS*. New York: Owl Books, 1993. A first-rate account of Himmler's role as one of the most destructive of the Nazi leaders.

Norman Polmar and Thomas B. Allen, *World War II: The Encyclopedia of the War Years 1941–1945*. New York: Random House, 1996. The ultimate resource on the war from an American perspective.

Reader's Digest Association, *Reader's Digest Illustrated Story of World*

War II. Pleasantville, NY: Reader's Digest Association, 1978. A collection of stories that together tell the tale of World War II.

William L. Shirer, *Berlin Diary: The Journal of a Foreign Correspondent, 1934–1941.* New York: Galahad Books, 1995. An eyewitness account of Europe in the last half of the 1930s and the early 1940s.

————, *The Rise and Fall of the Third Reich.* New York: Simon & Schuster, 1960. Still unmatched as the definitive history of Nazi Germany under Hitler.

Louis L. Snyder, *Encyclopedia of the Third Reich.* New York: Paragon House, 1989. A broad selection of historical data about Hitler and the Nazis.

Albert Speer, *Inside the Third Reich.* New York: Galahad Books, 1995. An engaging account of the Nazi inner circle by Hitler's armaments and production chief.

Time-Life Books editors, *The SS.* Vol. 2, The Third Reich series. Alexandria, VA: Time-Life Books, 1989. A lavishly illustrated and well-written chronicle of Hitler's elite force.

————, *WW II: Time-Life History of the Second World War.* New York: Barnes & Noble, 1995. A condensation of Time-Life's 39-volume series.

John Toland, *Adolf Hitler.* New York: Anchor Books, 1992. The definitive biography of the man who disrupted more lives and stirred more hatred than any other man.

Peter G. Tsouras, *Warrior's Words: A Quotation Book, from Sesostris III to Schwarzkopf, 1871 BC to AD 1991.* London: Arms and Armour Press, 1992. The words of more than 150 men of war.

Gerhard L. Weinberg, *Germany, Hitler, and World War II: Essays in Modern German and World History.* New York: Cambridge University Press, 1995. A collection of studies in twentieth-century German and world history.

John Weitz, *Hitler's Diplomat: The Life and Times of Joachim von Ribbentrop.* New York: Ticknor & Fields, 1992. An incisive account of Hitler's foreign minister and the social and political workings of Nazi Germany.

Leni Yahil, *The Holocaust: The Fate of European Jewry.* Translated by Ina Friedman and Haya Galai. New York: Oxford University Press, 1990. A sweeping look at the Final Solution, covering Nazi policies and how Jews and the world perceived them.

Index

Picture Credits

About the Author

Earle Rice Jr. attended San Jose City College and Foothill College on the San Francisco peninsula, after serving nine years with the United States Marine Corps.

He has authored more than thirty books for young adults, including fast-action fiction and adaptations of *Dracula, All Quiet on the Western Front,* and *The Grapes of Wrath.* Mr. Rice has written nineteen books for Lucent, including *The Cuban Revolution, The Salem Witch Trials, The Final Solution, Nazi War Criminals, Life in the Middle Ages, Kamikazes,* and seven books in the popular Great Battles series. He has also written articles, short stories, and miscellaneous website materials, and has previously worked for several years as a technical writer.

Mr. Rice is a former senior design engineer in the aerospace industry who now devotes full-time to his writing. The author is a member of the Society of Children's Book Writers and Illustrators (SCBWI); the League of World War I Aviation Historians and its UK-based sister organization, Cross & Cockade International; and the United States Naval Institute (USNI). He lives in Julian, California, with his wife, daughter, two granddaughters, and two cats.